The Green Stone

The Green Stone

Graham Phillips

Martin Keatman

(Jersey)
Neville Spearman

First published in Great Britain in 1983 by
Neville Spearman (Jersey) Limited.
P.O. Box 75, Normandy House, St. Helier,
Jersey, Channel Islands.

Distributed by Neville Spearman Limited
The Priory Gate, Friars Street,
Sudbury, Suffolk.

ISBN 0 85978 060 0

Typeset in 10/12 Palatino by
Witwell Limited, Liverpool.
Printed and bound in Great Britain by
Billings Ltd, Worcester.

For Mary

ACKNOWLEDGEMENTS

We should like particularly to thank Jean Astle, without whose help and encouragement this book could not have been written. We should also like to thank the following: Alan Beard, Penny Blackwill, Andrew Collins, Jane McKenzie, Peter Marlow, Janet Morgan, Jenny Randles, Mike Ratcliffe, Terry and Pat Shotton, Fred, Marion and Gaynor Sunderland, and all those — named and unnamed — who have assisted us in compiling this book.

Contents

Foreword by Jenny Randles

When I first encountered this astonishing story I reacted as I suppose anyone might. My senses reeled, and something sceptical that lurks within kept nagging at my brain. This cannot be, it insisted. It is always much easier to disregard truth than to face up to it; to sweep things under the carpet of life, especially when they push hard-won preconceptions into some remote corner of the cognisant universe.

As you read this absorbing and exciting tale of magic, mystery and adventure, you will perhaps be tempted to open up the filing cabinet in your mind which stores such things as fire-breathing dragons and more modern myths like *Star Wars* and *Lord of the Rings*. But resist that temptation. Try to think that this might actually have happened, and then ponder the consequences of these concessions to objectivity.

In principle, I regard myself as a fair-minded person. I am interested in scientific mysteries and unexplained anomalies, but I endeavour to keep my views in perspective. The result is that I tend to live in a kind of perpetual schizophrenia. On the one hand I sense a responsibility to my readers to present them with the truth about the world on the threshold of rationality, a truth they do not often see free of its customary distortion and sensationalism. Then, on the other hand, I have a responsibility to myself not to accept gullibly all the fantastic accounts that populate the landscapes of the paranormal. My books have attempted to display this dichotomy, and it is often far from easy.

And so, placing this incredible and epic adventure into some kind of rational context seems to defy possibility. For it is inherently irrational and yet oddly believable. That is perhaps the first thing which will strike you about this book. But, in a sense, I do have one other major advantage over the reader, I am outside this present-day fairy-tale. I do not have a role to play within it, yet I know all the people who are central to its action. And knowing them I find it much more difficult to dismiss as a hoax or fantasy.

Andy Collins was the first of the team I came to know. I met him as an eager teenage-researcher, some years back. He was already wise in the ways of mystery, but battling against the awe which accompanies everyone making their very first forrays into alien territory. I have watched him grow and evolve into a perceptive and cautious reporter, whilst still maintaining the blunt charm of his East London upbringing. If he says these things happened, then I have no valid motive to disbelieve him.

Martin Keatman I met a little later, in similar circumstances. He talks in a quick-fire way, rather like an express train going down hill. But his tumbling words usually echo clever insights and always mirror his insatiable enthusiasm. He coined the term 'acceptance level', where a witness to a paranormal phenomenon places his experience into a personally acceptable framework. I have constantly found this concept of value. In the time when Martin was an investigator (and journal editor) with the small band of truth-seekers I had the fortune to co-ordinate, I knew one thing with certainty. Ask Martin to do something and he would do it (indeed, quite probably already had done it!) His case reports were meticulous and detailed and I am sure he has applied this groundwork to the writing of this book.

Graham Phillips, through no fault of his, remains more of an enigma. Circumstances have contrived that we do not know each other as well as I would have liked. But each time I have met him, or seen his work in action, two things have struck me. One, is a sense of his subdued intelligence. By that I mean I *know* he is blessed with a surprising diversity of knowledge, and is capable of understanding more about the paradoxes that confront us daily. Yet he seems purposely to hide this sagacity beneath his rather more obvious character traits. Graham is a friendly chap, capable of putting anyone at ease, but at the same time selling them a hard line and thus bringing the best out of their performance.

It was interesting to watch these three, and their other colleagues, whom I met from time to time, as they slowly came together into the **Parasearch** team. Indeed, they seemed to be drawn into this almost mysteriously — rather like moths towards a candle flame. Their origins were different. Their personalities were incompatible. They formed a strange bunch of musketeers. But when they coalesced they became something very different. The whole *was* greater than its constituent parts. They formed a dynamic powerhouse of drive and enthusiasm which always seemed likely to make a major breakthrough. I am not surprised that they have done so.

Roles, like my non-existent one, seem important to the substance of this story. And it was Martin's role to act as a catalyst and coagulent. It was he who brought the team together. It was Martin, too, who while not appearing to have much of an active part to play in the adventure, first brought to the fore Marion and Gaynor Sunderland. For they knew him, and through his influence - plus a little serendipity — they were led towards the others and the completion of the circle. But even before this Martin had been integral.

By chance Paul Whetnall and I came across a small newspaper item from an un-named Welsh town, where an unknown girl had seen a UFO. I did not know how to find her, although the story seemed worth pursuing. Martin pointed the way by his fortuitous link with an isolated local investigator. The result was that Paul and I researched the first phase of the Sunderland saga and wrote a book about it. *Alien Contact** is in several respects a 'prequel' to this tale. For the incredible events which it portrays cannot be without relevance to those which were to follow and which led to the current quest. The first book concentrates on Marion, Gaynor and the rest of the Sunderland family. It shows how 'the unknown' literally homed in on a quiet coastal town, causing this family to experience more strange phenomena in a couple of years than the rest of us could expect in a lifetime. Martin, Andy and Graham took an interest in all of this, of course, and from the moment they met the Sunderlands there was a notable interaction. It was as if the final plug had gone into the socket, and the jump-switch thrown. The circuits buzzed. Power flowed. Something quite remarkable was set into motion.

It was possible to see these things happening. They were real. Whatever explanation one chooses to fit — like the facts in this new book — they cannot be denied. To dismiss them entirely is, of course, the reader's privilege. But it would be an act of failure. For denial of reality, unless one can prove it, must simply be an admission of defeat by the twin-horned army of prejudice and disbelief.

I do not know the meaning of this affair. Indeed, I suspect that the very act of discovery may be part of its purpose. Some years ago I used to teach — and I learnt one thing above everything else. Let's call it the primary directive of teaching. Never *tell* somebody how something works — give them the means and the incentive to find out for themselves.

From this point on we enter the realms of pure speculation. But this can be a crystal stream of enlightenment, if one does not lose oneself among the eddy currents. To remain aloof, never speculating, is not to drink of this spiritual refreshment. This has but one result ... dehydration of the soul.

At the end of *Alien Contact* I found myself still uncertain about the source of the 'contacts'. Was it something outside us — truly alien? Or was the alien within us — a deeper and wiser self which is triggered into being when the time is right? Since the Meonia contacts are really an extension of these earlier experiences, rather like a sharpening of psychic senses, the same question must again be asked. Yet I have a feeling, almost a foreboding, that the identification of the source itself is less important than identification of its purpose. And that purpose seems to connect with the future of our planet.

In 1975 I met a man called Gary who came from the Midlands. He talked about a mission and the importance of the *Heart of the Rose* ... a phrase to later occur in the Green Stone investigation. He quoted the prophecies of Nostradamus and spoke of a task which he had to perform. He, too, had been set on his way by a UFO contact. My encounter with Gary remains one of the most remarkable events in my past decade's research. In our book *UFOs: a British Viewpoint** Peter Warrington and I ventured some of our impressions. But there is much more. Gary is still here, seven years later, and he still insists that time is growing short.

There is a feeling rippling through humanity. It says that we are now within the 'End Times' ... and a serious bulletin of that name has even been created to study this movement. Biblical prophecies of Armageddon are seen by some to be drawing near. Many indicators seem to concur: physical, practical, philosophical and psychic. One can see a slow awakening of deeply-rooted fears. And this seems to be reflected in the world around us — both the world we like to think of as 'real', and the psychic world which some of us prefer to consider 'unreal'. I think that very soon we may be forced to heed these danger signals.

Here I must admit to another personal factor which perturbs me. I do not think that I am psychic, certainly not in the way that Gaynor or Graham seem to be. It could be that I am merely scared to admit that all of us are psychic. I know that. But I have had a number of dreams which, no matter how objectively I look at them, appear to have been precognitions. If I have a frequently recurring dream I suppose by now I ought to take notice. In fact, I have a strongly recurring dream. I have it a few times a month, sometimes twice a night. And it does not represent any emotions I consciously share to the same degree. This dream — which depicts a nuclear holocaust — has been with me for as long as I can remember — certainly since I was a young child. After twenty years I think I am entitled to treat my nightmare with a little respect.

The form for me is a recurring dream. For Gaynor it is a vision. And others receive different demonstrations of the same or a similar theme. Perhaps this is a sign of the times - a psychological by-product of a global mental illness. Or perhaps it is something more. In *Alien Contact* I called it a psychic alarm bell.

It is odd how this mood pervaded modern society. An effective monitor of the cultural aura is popular music. Songs dig deep into the unconscious of the writer and may stir into life those regions which are in touch with knowledge beyond time's hazy borders. What do we find in these songs? Words of war, death, the coming of the end, cosmic consciousness, alien salvation, and so on. Interestingly, a good deal of this concern displayed by human creativity oozes from the 'Heart of the Rose' or the English Midlands. The Moody Blues from Birmingham launched the cosmic rock revolution in 1968 and they still talk of our having to 'understand the voice within' so we can 'feel its power already beginning'. Not long ago they spoke of being 'frightened for our children ... that the sunshine we are waiting for will turn to rain' because 'when the final night is over (it will be) certain that the curtain's going to fall'. Toyah Wilcox has also impressed me with her plaintive, intense songs which take this same message onto a more obviously cosmic stage. She talks frequently of the aliens and their mission here, and believes what she sings about. And the Electric Light Orchestra (*ELO*), who also stem from the Midlands, had a best-selling album in 1981 which gave the story of a man who is abducted by his own dreams to awake in a frightening future. After seeing the consequences of today's foolishness he is sent back to offer a warning ... 'return with what you've learnt. They'll kiss the ground you walk upon.' It cannot be without meaning that this kind of music and these artists who create it are enormously popular in the eighties.

Fantasy fiction is showing the same trend. Stephen Donaldson's trilogy, *The Chronicles of Thomas Covenant* have had an unprecedented success, converting millions the world over with its Tolkeinist images. These three epic novels, and the second trilogy which Donaldson is producing, concern a man of this world, Thomas Covenant, and later a female compatriot, Linden Avery, who travel to 'The Land', a magic world of forests, rivers and mountains where men of all breeds dwell with giants and mythical humanoids. Anyone who reads this fiction as well as *Alien Contact* and *The Green Stone* cannot fail to be impressed by the remarkable correspondances. It is almost as if Donaldson and the authors of these books were tapping the same source — the difference being that the American author clothes the images in fictional terms and the *Parasearch* team actually go on and *live* them!

The Covenant books involve a war between good and evil — Armageddon. Covenant is summoned to wield his influence and with a band of followers sets off on the lengthy quest. There is a green jewel-like stone (the Illearth Stone) around which the battle rages. There is a small sword, too, which is cast into a lake so that it may not be used, but is later retrieved to become a powerful symbol. Covenant and Avery are abducted to the land in a very similar way to which Gaynor Sunderland and others claim in *Alien contact.*

There is, of course, much more to the synchronicity than this. But this taster makes evident my essential point. These Covenant books *were* quite independent. They were published after the *events* which make up *Alien Contact* and part of *The Green Stone* had taken place, but before the publication of both books. If you have been captivated by their strange compulsion you need only read on to confront the reality behind them.

The enormous and surprising popularity of the Donaldson books, the success of music such as that I have mentioned, the interest and incidence of prediction and prophecy, all makes it seem as if something is trying to impart a rather special message of great urgency and impact, and one which we must try to understand now.

Maybe that is the point. Perhaps, after all, my speculations have presented me with a role. It seems necessary to indicate the apparent existence of this cultural tidal wave. And if I am on target then the extraordinary drama which you are about to read demonstrates a most important dilemma. We may wish to ignore it — but can we really afford to? On its understanding might lie the fate of human civilisation. And this is something with which we must never take chances.

Birchwood
Cheshire
June 1982.

Alien Contact. Neville Spearman, 1982.
UFOs: a British Viewpoint, Robert Hale, 1979.

Authors' Note

The account you are about to read may sound fantastic and unbelievable, but it is true. All the events occurred just as we have presented them. The witnesses to these events stand to lose much by admitting to having been involved in something so unorthodox, and it is for this reason that we must explain why this book has been written.

Throughout the period concerned, many of those who found themselves involved hoped that others would not need to know about what was taking place. However, as time progressed, more and more people either became directly drawn into or got to know something of the events. It was therefore unavoidable that some parts of the story received media coverage and, as the phenomena continued, so did the interest.

In retrospect it was perhaps short-sighted of us to have imagined that the lid would remain sealed for long on such a story. It was inevitable that, sooner or later, something would find its way into print. Eventually, when fragmentary accounts were presented, either as short features or newsworthy items, they sometimes misrepresented what was actually taking place. In addition, distorted word of mouth accounts and various individual ideas about what was responsible for the affair also brought about some very peculiar versions. We realised then that only a straightforward and full account told by those involved would minimise the problems that could be foreseen.

Chapter One

———◆———

The Chosen

NOVEMBER 22, 1875. The barking of a dog echoed faintly in the distance. Outside the rising wind blew through the trees. But this was no time for listening to familiar night sounds. Seven people, seven diverse backgrounds, all aware that for them the cold light of morning might never come. Soon their lonely vigil would be over.

The solitary gas lamp hissed and flickered, breaking the uneasy silence in the darkened room. A whisp of pipe smoke revealed a bearded old man sitting motionless and silent on an old oak chair. About him six others, shadowy indefinable figures waiting patiently for the inevitable.

Anxious eyes fell on the old man as he rose and shuffled over to the heavy iron stove. Opening the buckled door he knocked his pipe against the metal, the glow from the dying embers of the fire casting eerie shadows around the room. The red light reflecting from row after row of bottled potions and chemicals on the dusty shelves.

Time was short. This they all knew. Repeatedly they had tried to destroy the power that threatened them. But now they must finally face that power. They would not trouble the old man, for the burden of decision lay heavy on his shoulders. He alone would decide their fate.

After a time he turned and spoke. 'Friends, we can wait no longer. The time has come, we must do what must be done.' He glanced down at his gold pocket watch. 'A quarter past eleven. We must make ready.' He fell silent, eyes slowly closing as if to allow time for his proclamation to take hold. A tense silence fell upon the group.

This time there would be no escaping the confrontation.

A sudden ring broke the silence. The doorbell. The party cast anxious glances towards the old man. He gestured his hand to command quiet, kindling one of the oil lamps and picking a slow but deliberate path between them. He made his way along the narrow passage into the front room of the house.

Nervously he opened the door. Before him stood two figures, a man and a woman. In the darkness he recognised her, a tall, elegant woman in her late twenties. Next to her stood a shorter man of similar age wearing a heavy tweed coat. The woman looked distressed. Through the light of the oil lamp her swollen eyes betrayed the recent tears. Clasped to her breast she held a short rectangular wooden box. And then the old man knew.

She strode forward into the room, pulling off her bonnet and releasing her long, brown hair. 'What has happened?' asked the old man. He knew as well as they, but could not, did not want to believe it.

At last she spoke. 'We must act now and we must act quickly. With each passing moment our chances diminish as their power grows.' The man said nothing. Momentarily he raised his head and nodded in agreement. The old man sighed. His decision had been made for him. Only the two of them had come, and she had brought the box.

The three made their way down the corridor into the back room. 'My friends,' the old man announced, 'the decision had been made for me. We are now in the hands of God, he alone can help us.' In silent unison the assembly rose and lit the remaining oil lamps, filing almost reverently along the corridor leading to the cellar entrance. The old man crouched, pulling aside the heavy wooden panel. A rush of cold air struck their faces as the door was lifted, the dank smell of the underground chamber reaching out as they descended the sand-covered steps.

The lamps quickly filled the room with shimmering light, unveiling four white walls richly adorned with ancient symbols: the ankh, the winged sun disc. Upon the floor a large eight-pointed star painted in white. At each point stood an earthenware plate containing sand. Adjacent to each plate was a phial of water. The group lit candles and placed them between the water and the sand. Earth, Air, Fire and Water. The circle was complete.

Quickly they adopted their rightful positions around the star, each to one of the eight points, the young woman in the centre. No-one spoke. The ritual had begun.

From the box the woman withdrew a short sword. The candles flickered and danced, casting long shadows on the mystic symbols adorning the walls. She gripped the hilt of the weapon and thrust it high above her head. The watchers linked hands. They could not take their eyes off the woman, radiant in her passion, about to give everything for their cause.

As if guided by some unseen signal their eyes closed simultaneously. They must visualize, concentrate their energies upon her. Around her they focussed a sphere of mental energy; white, protective, pure. Through the silence she began to speak, softly and to herself, muttering words in some long forgotten language. All seemed well.

Her words became louder, more frenzied. Silently they urged her on, feeding their minds into hers. A sudden discordant tone resonated through the room, like a high pitched scream, intensifying, echoing, piercing the fragile atmosphere. It seemed to come from far away, like glass, falling slowly, shattering onto yet more glass. It came louder with each passing second.

But still she spoke, her words louder, more intense, until finally she was screaming in competition with the unearthly sound. Now she was crying silently, her mental anguish manifesting physically. Her lips parted slightly, but no words came. Throwing back her head she screamed horribly, the muscles knotted across her neck and shoulders. Simultaneously the noise mounted to a deafening crescendo, tearing the room apart with a sheer wall of sound and hurling the candles from the circle into blackness. Instantly it stopped. Only her screams shattered the darkness.

A pinprick of white light snapped on only a yard above her head. Gleaming in the blackness, pulsating rhythmically but casting no light into the chamber. But still she gripped the sword, her tortured face wet with tears. Her screams subsided into silent weeping. Seconds passed.

Again she chanted, and again they poured their strength into her body. The white sphere continued to grow, pulsating in the blackness. The atmosphere was thick and warm; slowly but unstoppably it grew thicker and hotter, drying the sweat from their hands, the saliva from their mouths.

3

Suddenly there was a terrible cry. The woman slumped to the floor as the sword was ripped viciously from her hands and hurled against the steps by some unseen force. An overpowering stench tortured their nostrils; oppressive and pungent it clawed at their stomachs.

In the light they saw a figure, black and cold, bearing down on the woman. She twitched involuntarily and began to move, slowly and painfully, clutching at the empty air as if searching for some handhold.

They could not help her. To break the circle meant certain death. The dishevelled figure struggled to her feet, jerking her head back and emitting a shrill cry as she stabbed her arms at the dark assailant looming overhead. Nothing. The cold shadow seethed in the light as if in mocking response.

Her voice broke painfully into their ears. 'I have failed us in our time of greatest need.' She gulped violently. 'My ... our power is spent, all is lost.' The presence grew, wiping away the light around it as she spoke. 'Go, quickly, take the sword from this place and hide it well. Let it guide those who will surely come, let them succeed in the quest where we have failed.'

The last vestiges of light faded rapidly from the cellar, leaving only impenetrable blackness.

'Let *them* possess the *Meonia Stone*.'

4

Chapter Two

———◆———

New Beginnings

SUMMER 1979. During the late summer of 1979, a number of men, women and children throughout Great Britain received remarkably similar, strange psychic messages that were to bring them together for possibly the strangest quest in history, a quest to discover a mysterious green stone, and with it unlock the darkest secret of the ancient world.

It all began on a quiet autumn evening in 1974, when the Avis family from Essex were travelling along a lonely country road near their home in Aveley. A strange, blue light manoeuvered in the sky before them and dropped from sight below the horizon. Seconds later they rounded a corner bordered by tall hedges and coasted into a bank of cold green mist lying across the road. They emerged over two hours later and a mile further on. They could not account for the lost time.

Over the following three years, however, both John and Sue Avis began to have strange, sometimes unnerving dreams. Household items began to move or be thrown inexplicably across the front room. Throbbing electronic noises, bangs and mysterious scratchings were heard by various members of the family, and on at least one occasion a dark humanoid figure was seen in the living room.

But even more amazingly, if their story was to be believed, the family developed marked signs of extrasensory perception in the months and years following their encounter with the green mist.

In 1977, Andrew Collins and Barry King, both Essex based UFO investigators, interviewed the parents. On discovering the time loss of over two hours the pair sought the aid of hypnotherapist Leonard Wilder, since possibly hypnosis would be of value in prompting a recall of the lost time.

Whilst under hypnosis John Avis claimed to recall having been taken aboard a strange, alien craft and subjected to a medical examination by its tall occupants clad in one-piece silver suits. Sue Avis later recalled the same experience, although she was never hypnotised.

As Andrew Collins investigated this remarkable claim, he became increasingly convinced that there was some link between the apparent UFO abduction and the paranormal events that subsequently occurred. These paranormal experiences included a series of particularly lucid dreams and psychic impressions about future events. Amongst other information the Avis's were given, seemingly by the alien intelligence that had abducted them, was that a group of people would shortly come together to perform certain important tasks involving a mysterious psychic conflict sometime in the future. The information was fantastic and unbelievable, but Andy and Barry recorded it for future reference. (1)

In October 1978, while talking to parapsychologist Graham Phillips, an ex-serviceman John Ward related virtually identical psychic information. A remarkably accurate psychic from Stourbridge in Worcestershire, Ward had experienced strange vivid dreams and had also developed the peculiar ability of astral projection. (2) He too had claimed that a nucleus of people would soon be brought together in Central England by some mysterious intelligence, and would be involved in an important quest ultimately leading to a confrontation with something beyond their understanding. Unlike John and Sue, however, John Ward felt his visions to be inspired by his religious beliefs.

By this time Graham Phillips had met Andrew Collins and Barry King through their mutually shared interest in the paranormal. On comparing notes they discovered the uncanny similarity between the two sets of messages, and, although perplexed by this, they decided to reserve judgement while awaiting further developments.

The Avis family investigations concluded, Andy and Barry continued to research other encounters where a link between UFOs and paranormal phenomena appeared to exist. Graham accompanied them on several of these inquiries. Later that year the three founded an organisation to investigate the increasingly apparent links between many kinds of unexplained phenomena. By early 1979, the organisation was established, and working under the name *Parasearch*. In order to help finance their investigations they published a news-stand magazine from Graham's flat. His apartment in Oaks Crescent, Wolverhampton, was now doubling as the *Parasearch* office and headquarters.

Through his interest in the paranormal and the magazine, UFO and paranormal investigator Martin Keatman contacted Phillips and Collins and joined the organisation.

Over the August Bank Holiday weekend of 1979 the three researchers attended the first International UFO Congress at the Mount Royal Hotel in London. UFO researchers from as far afield as the U.S.A. and Italy had gathered to share their latest findings and attend a packed three days of lectures and debates, official dinners and less formal gatherings.

On the Sunday, Martin introduced Graham and Andy to Mrs Marion Sunderland, a mother of five living in the suburban village of Oakenholt just outside Flint in North Wales. In the hot summer of 1976, her daughter Gaynor, then aged nine, was riding her bicycle along the quiet country lane near their home when she saw something she would never forget.

Out of the corner of her eye she suddenly caught a glint of silver in an open field to her left. Clambering off her bike and peering through the hedge she was confronted by a large, oval-shaped object, motionless and silent in the field before her.

The mysterious craft was about thirty feet across and shone a metallic silver in the sunlight.

Two humanoid figures, one male and one female, clad in one-piece silver suits and close-fitting, balaclava-like helmets, emerged from behind the object and appeared to take samples of soil from the field.

As the female entity looked up into the sky Gaynor took her opportunity to escape. She scrambled out of the ditch where she was lying, grabbed her bicycle and, dragging it behind her, ran as best she could along the lane back towards her home.

Glancing behind her she saw the UFO climbing into the sky, until it was lost from sight in the only cloud to be seen on that hot, summer day.

Martin had been investigating this fascinating UFO sighting by Gaynor. Even before this encounter it seemed that she was psychic. She could see the human aura and had even shown certain telepathic abilities. Still more strange was that in the months and years following her main UFO experience in 1976 she said she had maintained contact with these alien beings. So it was that Marion Sunderland, her mother, became interested in UFOs. In the years subsequent to Gaynor's sighting she was catapulted into a terrifyingly new situation, where literally all her five children claimed to have witnessed some form of strange, paranormal phenomena. (3)

Her growing interest had prompted her to search for answers and discover more about what lay behind her children's UFO and psychic experiences. For this reason she had decided to attend the conference in the hope that someone might be able to offer advice.

As Martin and Marion discussed her family's situation it quickly became evident that it was in many ways similar to the Avis family's following their 1974 UFO abduction.

Martin introduced Marion to Andy and Graham, hoping that the results of their research into a case similar to hers might provide her with some of the answers she was seeking.

The four talked for some time, discussing the apparent links between UFOs and psychic phenomena. Marion had found it difficult to accept that her children could have seen such bizarre things as UFOs and their entities. The three investigators assured her that such experiences could and did occur with frightening regularity to sane and sensible people from all over the world. Marion discussed her feelings at some length, saying how she still did not know what to make of it all. Half an hour later she excused herself and headed for the conference room.

And there matters would probably have rested, had it not been for the next ten, eventful minutes.

Marion Sunderland suddenly reappeared, looking somehow different. She was staring fixedly at Andy and she did not take her eyes off him as she approached.

Martin and Graham fell silent. Andy stopped as they did, looked at them and turned to see Marion Sunderland staring directly at him. She stopped and opened her mouth as if to speak, then checked herself. A moment of silence followed. Marion appeared to become conscious of the situation and shook her head in bewilderment.

'I'm sorry,' she said with an uneasy smile, 'but I ...' she paused to glance at Graham and Martin. 'I hope you're not going to think I'm crazy or anything, but, well I wasn't going to say. . . .

'What is it?' asked Martin.

'Have you met any clairvoyants or mediums?' she asked with a frown.

'Quite a few,' answered Graham. 'Why?'

'Well, I'm not clairvoyant, not in the true sense of the word, I suppose, but I have had what you might call psychic impressions about people and places that have later turned out to be accurate.' She paused and looked at Andy. 'As I said, I wasn't going to say anything in case I appeared foolish. After all, I'm trying my hardest not to throw any doubt on my children in discussing the paranormal.' She fell quiet again as they stared at her blankly. 'Andy,' she said, 'it was with you when I was talking to you earlier.'

'What was?' he asked.

'It was like agitated hands. I could see in my mind's eye, very vividly, a woman with agitated hands.' She stopped and shrugged. 'That's the best way I can describe it. A woman trying to warn you.'

'Warn me?' said Andy, puzzled. 'Warn me about what?'

'You must think I'm silly, but is there a woman somewhere who wants to put money into your magazine, quite a large sum?'

Andy's mouth dropped open as he stared back at her. 'Go on,' he urged.

'I don't think you should accept it,' she said slowly. 'At least, that's the feeling I get. I think there's something very wrong.'

The questioning looks of the three investigators prompted her to add more. 'I don't know what it is, but I think you've got to be careful, very careful. There is something you ...' She paused before continuing. 'Your group, there is something very important.' She shook her head. 'I don't understand it.' She appeared to be straining her eyes and ears, all her senses to hear, to see something around her. She continued hesitantly. 'Please don't think I'm crazy, but I've never felt anything like it before. It's almost as if you are all involved in something, something which has only just begun.'

Puzzled glances were exchanged as she elaborated. 'You're involved in something you don't understand. There is something you must do.' Marion seemed rather embarrassed and hurriedly bid them farewell. 'I'm sorry I've taken up your time,' she said. 'I'll have to be off, or I'll miss the next lecture.'

Her psychic impression was quite astounding. Unknown to Marion, in the weeks and months leading up to the conference, five psychics had independently warned them that a woman Andy Collins knew was not to be trusted. An offer of finance she made for the magazine should not be accepted they had said. Until that Sunday in August Andy had puzzled over this, but now his decision had been made. In all, six psychics had warned him, and that was enough. Stranger still, here was yet another person, this time known only to Martin, who had told *Parasearch* that there was some important task they must soon undertake. Since Marion Sunderland's message had been so accurate, they now decided that maybe, just maybe, there was some substance in the other messages they had been receiving.

That night they talked hard and long, but by the late evening they had again decided to reserve making a final judgement.

With the conference over Andy and Graham resumed work on the magazine. One evening Graham arrived back at the Wolverhampton *Parasearch* headquarters and took a telephone call from Terry Shotton, a Midland-based UFO investigator and paranormal researcher.

Terry explained how he had visited a Staffordshire medium named Penny Blackwill to investigate her paranormal experiences. During their conversation she had fallen quiet, and after a short time declared that she was sure something was about to happen to Terry. Having witnessed the accuracy of some of her previous psychic impressions he was somewhat concerned. She said that he was shortly to become involved with something she could not understand, something that involved him, members of *Parasearch* and still others to come. She added that in the early autumn of 1979 the first stages of this task would begin. Graham and Terry discussed at length this and the other messages, and were led to the conclusion that maybe something very strange *was* about to occur to the organisation.

As the week following Terry's unexpected call unfolded, there followed further calls of a similar nature. The psychics involved were known to Andy and Graham through the work of *Parasearch* and the magazine; to their astonishment they all reported similar messages to those given by the Avis's, John Ward, Marion Sunderland and Penny Blackwill.

Yvonne Parry, a well-known London spiritualist, had phoned to speak to Graham, and in the course of conversation said she felt there was something that *Parasearch* would soon become involved with, something of great importance. However, she, too, was at a loss to explain further.

The summer months of 1979 had thus set *Parasearch* on a new path of inquiry. People from all over the country receiving a psychic message concerning the organisation and a task or quest which it would soon undertake. What was this mysterious task? None of them seemed to know. But as the days passed an uneasy apprehension descended on those concerned as they waited patiently for some indication that these strange psychic messages, all so similar and all from people previously unknown to one another, were in some way real.

From an objective, paranormal research point of view, it was intriguing that all the psychics had received what was basically the same message, but they had all had different paranormal experiences: mediumship, a UFO abduction, a close encounter of the third kind, and an apparently religious experience. Somehow they had all received the same message, but a message from allegedly completely different sources. The intimation was obvious. Was this message, this hint of things to come, from only one supernatural agency, using the available beliefs of the pyschics? The evidence certainly pointed that way. But if this was so, *what was this intelligence*?

Chapter Three

———◆———

Revelations

AUTUMN 1979. In mid-September Andy accepted Marion's invitation to visit the Sunderland family in their north Wales home. It was a hunch really, an intuitive feeling he had known before. The feeling that a witness or psychic may know more than they are saying. This, plus his desire to hear at first hand the stories of the UFO and psychic experiences.

Over the weekend he took time to get to know them, to discuss their thoughts and feelings as a family confronted with the unexplained.

On the Sunday he sat in the living room talking to Marion and her husband Fred. All day Marion had felt that something might happen. Following her intuition she had led them to a nearby field, where her children had frequently experienced strange presences and sensations. The trip was, however, uneventful and they returned to the warmth of the house to talk.

Fred didn't say a lot, he preferred to sit and listen. The ease with which he had accepted the bizarre claims and experiences of his family was a good sign. From the outset he had remained objective, calmly accepting Marion's growing interest and the visitors who came to talk to her about UFOs. He was unable to explain what had occurred, or what his children had seen, and until he could do so he would maintain an open mind.

By now it was late evening. Upstairs the children were sound asleep. Only the voices of Andy and Marion broke the silence. Suddenly Andy saw a flash of white light as an object arched through the air and splintered in half on the gasfire before falling onto the carpet.

'It's Darren's tooth!' cried Fred.

Earlier that day their son Darren had lost a milk tooth and had put it on the mantlepiece for safe keeping. It had somehow projected of it's own accord and broken on the fire.

All three of them had seen it, of that they were certain. They searched for an answer. Maybe a passing vehicle had vibrated the tooth in such a way as to dislodge it, or heat from the fire had caused it to expand and subsequently move. Although they searched for a plausible explanation, none was forthcoming. There was simply no way it could have jumped with such power.

Andy left Marion's more puzzled than ever. Could it have been a trick, a hoax to impress him? No, he could not see Marion or Fred doing that, and anyway, what could they hope to achieve by such a pointless act. In the back of his mind he was concerned. For the first time in his life he had witnessed what seemed to be a geniune poltergeist event. And that first time had been at the home of Marion Sunderland, the self-same women who had provided him and *Parasearch* with two uncannily accurate psychic messages. Maybe there was more to it. The tooth episode had set him thinking. There was only one way to find out: a second visit.

★ ★ ★ ★

The late afternoon sun streamed in through the living-room window. Outside Marion's children bounded playfully across the *cul-de-sac*, amusing themselves in the safety of the secluded close.

Graham, Andy and Martin sat talking to Marion as she explained how her family's experiences had prompted her to try and contact any mother in a similar position. To this end she had featured in a series of local newspaper stories which requested other parents to come forward. (1) To her surprise a considerable number of people from the Flint area claimed similar experiences to Gaynor's. Most were children or teenagers, and some even claimed to have had encounters around the same time as her daughter's in July 1976.

The *Parasearch* investigations had revealed an intriguing fact, that at least four close encounters of the third kind had occurred less than five miles from the site of Gaynor's meeting with the landed UFO and its occupants. This in itself was surprising, since it was rare to find so heavy a concentration of UFO encounters involving occupants within so small an area.

That weekend Fred was away with the Territorial Army and they spoke openly to Marion, uncertain if she had told Fred or wanted him to know about her impressions concerning Andy and *Parasearch* at the conference. When asked for an explanation she seemed embarrassed at the prospect of recall, but after some hesitation explained how she had felt there was something powerful, some mysterious force which she could not explain acting to make the woman inject finance into the magazine.

'What kind of force?' asked Graham.

'I don't know, but I . . . for a moment felt it at the conference,' she said. 'I've never felt anything like it before. It was wrong, very wrong.'

She fell silent and said no more. The three took the opportunity to change the subject, drawing Marion away from something it seemed she really did not want to remember. The question of visiting some of the UFO witnesses who had written to her was broached. She voiced no objections, and it was agreed that they would investigate one of the letters she had received. Gaynor had expressed an interest in meeting other children who claimed to have seen UFOs, and asked Marion and the investigators if she could go along. They all agreed.

On the Sunday afternoon they drove to the holiday resort of Prestatyn to visit a concerned mother, while Graham stayed behind to watch over the children in Marion's absence. The woman's seven year-old daughter said she had seen a UFO with multicoloured lights crossing the sky over her house. The object had emitted a strange buzzing sound and hovered above a car in the road outside. The girl's claim was substantiated by her mother who had also heard the mysterious buzzing.

At first she was worried by her daughter's experience, but as she and Marion talked her fears faded, and she seemed glad to have the sympathetic ear of someone who understood what it was like to have normal children claiming abnormal experiences.

Martin questioned several neighbours as Andy busied himself taking photographs of the site. Gaynor tagged along, occasionally asking questions and making her own observations. A sudden change came over her as she stood next to Martin. Her

15

smile dropped. She became subdued as if far away, staring into the sky at the rooftops opposite the girl's house. Martin followed her gaze but saw nothing. She appeared to be watching something above the houses, her eyes travelling slowly from right to left. Martin alerted Marion and nodded silently towards Gaynor.

'What is it?' he whispered, not wanting to break her concentration. At first she did not seem to hear. He felt he was with a stranger; her face wore the expression of someone much older.

'They're here,' she said quietly. 'Over there.' She gestured towards the rooftops. Martin strained his eyes, seeing nothing but an impenetrable bank of rain clouds scudding across the sky.

'What can you see?'

'Nothing ... but I know ... I can feel them.' She turned towards him. He was staring straight into her eyes, not the eyes of the little girl he knew. They seemed deep, knowing, almost a darker blue than usual. He felt uneasy. Something was happening, something only Gaynor could perceive.

As quickly as she had suddenly changed she was her normal self again. Her eyes stared up at him and blinked as she smiled.

'Can you describe what you saw?' said Marion, as she walked over.

'Nope,' came the simple characteristic reply, and without a care in the world she skipped off to join her new-found friend.

Before they left Flint Marion told them how she felt sure that Gaynor's UFO experience was in some way connected with what was happening, and that the presences they both sometimes felt near them were attempting to communicate something important. Although she did not say so, she gave the distinct impression that she believed these presences were one and the same as those that had imparted the message to the various psychics.

They were finding it increasingly difficult to account for the bizarre series of messages. Was something really about to happen? Could the psychics be right? Logic and common sense said no, but still they could not help feeling most uneasy about the whole thing.

On Friday, October 12, Martin arrived at the *Parasearch* office in Oaks Crescent. Earlier that day over the phone Andy had explained to him how something very odd had happened, something that threw new light on the situation.

'Take a look at these,' he said, leaning forward across the table and opening his briefcase. 'If you had some hard evidence that one, just one, of the psychics involved was somehow in communication with an intelligence would you be more inclined to accept these messages?'

'Of course,' answered Martin, 'but I think it's highly unlikely we'd ever find such evidence.'

'You're right. It is highly unlikely, but take a look at these.' He reached into his briefcase and took out a thin negative holder. He slid out a strip of six and passed them across the table.

'The photographs I took of the houses opposite that little girl's house in Prestatyn,' he stated.

Martin held the strip up into the light. Above the rooftops, on the two frames in question, he could cearly make out a distinct white mark on the negatives.

'What on earth are they?' Martin exclaimed. 'There must be dust or something on the film.'

Andy took two prints of the negatives from his bag and passed them over. 'God knows,' he said.

On the first was the clearly defined image of a dark circular mass with what appeared to be two lights on it. The second was the same scene from a different angle. On this was an even clearer image of a dark elongated oval shape. The object, whatever it was, seemed slightly higher in the sky and had no light patches on it like the first.

Andy explained how he had shown the prints and negatives to an acquaintance, a photographic technician attached to the radiology department of the local hospital, who had been unable to explain the images.

'Unless there's some other answer,' said Andy, 'they appear to be photographs of the same object ... at a different angle and position in the sky.'

Martin shook his head slowly, struggling to find a solution, torn between doubt and the chance that possibly they did indeed show something strange and inexplicable. He could not forget that they were taken exactly where Gaynor had said she felt the presences and at almost exactly the same time. Although Gaynor

17

had seen nothing she had said 'her friends' were there, a reference to the supposed aliens which she still claimed contact with since her close encounter. If the pictures were as they seemed, then Gaynor really had sensed the presence of some alien intelligence that Sunday afternoon, and it had been captured on film. (2)

Andy had phoned Marion to tell her about the photographs and found she was only mildly surprised by them. She explained how she had felt that something like this would happen to substantiate the psychic messages.

Until then it had been psychic messages, impressions, which, although fascinating and baffling in themselves, were not objective, solid evidence. The photographs threw new light on things, and if they were as they seemed then this was actual evidence that the strange happenings and messages were real. But how had the images appeared on the photographs? A camera cannot record something that is not there, and certainly no-one had seen anything in the sky above the rooftops as they followed Gaynor's stare that afternoon.

The investigators had, it appeared, photographed something totally unexplained. But what did these pictures show: a strange alien craft? Or was it perhaps something even further beyond imagination?

After they had discussed the photographs for some time, Andy told Martin about something still more bizarre which had taken place the previous evening. He had been talking with Graham and another friend, a local paranormal researcher called Stephen.

Stephen explained how he had achieved some interesting results in increasing concentration and psychic abilities by using meditational techniques. For the purposes of furthering their research the three decided to test these simple breathing exercises.

Everything was going according to plan when Graham suddenly lapsed into a strange state. Andy appealed to Stephen for help, but he had mysteriously fallen asleep and despite all his efforts Andy was unable to rouse him. After a few moments Graham fell completely silent and appeared to have stopped breathing. Thinking he may have suffered some form of seizure Andy was about to phone the doctor when Graham began to whisper. At first Andy could not distinguish the words, but after a short time they became clearer and slightly louder.

He appeared to have fallen into some kind of trance and a secondary personality was speaking through him. Andy was shocked, since Graham was not a medium and had never before fallen into trance. Stranger still was that the voice did not claim to be the spirit of a departed soul, but a living person; a woman calling herself Joanna who claimed to be at that very moment alive and living somewhere in England.

This voice, this Joanna, told Andy that the psychic impressions people had been having were connected with an important task that must soon be undertaken. This was the culmination of events which had begun centuries ago with the Egyptian Pharoah Akhenaten during the early fourteenth century B.C. When Joanna said she must leave, Graham awoke, remembering nothing of what had occurred. At first he even thought Andy was having him on, believing he had merely fallen asleep. Andy assured him he had not, and to prove it played Graham the tape recording he had made. Much to Andy's surprise it had not recorded, except for a short section at the beginning, and this was strangest of all.

Andy switched on the tape for Martin to listen to. For a few seconds there was silence before Graham's voice broke in loud and clear. It sounded as if the voice, although only a whisper, was echoing through a large hall. Over and over it slowly repeated the name *Akhenaten* until after several repetitions it gradually faded. Andy explained how at no time during the trance had Graham repeated the name Akhenaten in this way.

Along with the messages and evidence of the photographs there was now this, Graham falling into a trance and a voice speaking through him claiming to be a living woman.

'So you're the only witness,' said Martin.

'Yes, that's why I want you with me tonight,' answered Andy. 'Joanna said she was coming back...'

CHAPTER FOUR

Remember, Remember…

ANDY and Martin discussed this latest development with Graham, who found it very difficult to accept that he had fallen into an involuntary trance during which a mysterious voice had spoken through him. They talked for hours, but still they could not resolve what had taken place the previous evening.

At around 9.00 p.m. Andy suggested that Graham lie down and attempt the meditation exercise once again, since both of them felt it was this which in some way had prompted the episode. Graham lay on the couch and relaxed as Andy readied his cassette. A second recorder was to be used in case Andy's failed to record again. At Graham's request the lights were dimmed.

For some minutes there was silence. Only Graham's deep rhythmic breathing could be heard in the darkened room. After a time he began to breathe more quickly, more irregularly. His head began to turn from side to side.

'Andy,' Martin whispered, 'are you sure he's okay?'

'It's the same as last night,' he whispered back, gesturing for Martin to be silent.

Graham's body relaxed, leaving him motionless and silent. The two waited in the darkness, tense and nervous.

Seconds passed, and Graham showed no signs of breathing. Andy drew nearer. Martin's heart beat faster, his body reacting to the fear he felt. The silence was broken as Graham began to breathe again, deeply and regularly. Still he made no signs of movement.

'Joanna?' said Andy apprehensively.

21

'Yes,' came the whispered reply.

'D'you mind us trying to contact you again?'

'It was meant to happen this way,' answered the whispering voice. 'I have a great deal to explain to you.'

'Is Graham coming to any harm by you speaking through him?'

'No harm at all. Please do not worry, no harm will be allowed to befall him.'

'Are you sure?' queried Andy.

'He may be a little tired, but nothing more.' Joanna reassured him.

Martin and Andy sat next to the couch in silence, transfixed as the voice spoke without interruption for over half an hour. As he spoke they noticed slight inflexions in the voice which made it sound unfamiliar.

Could they possibly be listening to the words of a woman at that very moment alive somewhere on earth, or was the voice a secondary personality of Graham's? They simply did not know.

Joanna was relating a fascinating historical saga which began in ancient Egypt some 3,000 years ago.

At that time the country was ruled by the brilliant, but inexperienced Pharaoh Amonhotep IV, a dreamy but well-meaning young man whom fate had decreed to govern one of the most powerful nations on earth.

It was to this man that the leaders of a race once great but now in decline looked as a beneficiary to their own great wisdom. They saw in Amonhotep the qualities of one who could infuse their knowledge, not only into his nation but into the entire civilized world; by reason, argument and example, and not by force, which they found abhorrent.

This dying race were the Megalithic peoples of Britain and Northern Europe, a race whose greatest achievements were the impressive monuments of Stonehenge and the Avebury stone circle. Joanna claimed that these peoples had possessed great wisdom which had eventually been misused.

So it was that the last guardians of their secret knowledge journeyed to the civilized lands of the Middle East, trusting their wisdom to Amonhotep who founded a new religion based on belief in the existence of only one God. It was then that he changed his name to Akhenaten to display his conversion.

This new religion was so unpopular to many in Akhenaten's

Egypt that it divided the nation. The King therefore built a new city, a centre of learning where his devotees could practise unhindered their beliefs and new way of life. Akhenaten eventually moved his court to this new city, so isolating himself further from many of his subjects.

After his death those living in the new city were outlawed when the old religion, a belief in many gods, was reinstated.

Judging their situation as inevitably hopeless, Akhenaten's successors mounted a quest to leave Egypt and travel northwards in search of the land from where their knowledge had originated. This they did, apparently reaching Britain in the last decade of the fourteenth century B.C.

And so, in the cold, damp forests of Central England, they founded a new colony to follow the old lore. In the course of time the colony expanded, as a number of the early Celtic migrants from Europe joined them.

At the heart of the colony they built a hill-fort to defend themselves and their culture against surrounding hostile tribes. Joanna claimed that the remains of this ancient fort could still be seen today. Then, some centuries later, the descendants of this colony were threatened by hostile northern tribes and so appointed a leader, a woman named Gwevaraugh, who became a great and successful warrior queen, so much so that many of the other surrounding tribes became annexed to them. After her death Gwevaraugh, her chief councillors and war lords, who had done so much to permanently establish the lore, became the heroes of legends, and in certain communities around Britain rewritten and altered versions of these stories formed the basis of later written accounts that eventually became integrated into some of the Celtic romances and legends.

Gwevaraugh became known as Gwenhwyfar, a legendary warrior queen, who, in later times, was demoted in myth to Guinevere, the wife of King Arthur.

The secret knowledge taught by Akhenaten and Gwevaraugh passed through the Roman occupation of Britain and the subsequent Dark Ages as a secret, inner lore known only to a few, whom Joanna referred to as *The Nine*, dwelling somewhere in Central England. Joanna did not fully explain everything from this point, but said there was much that they would eventually

23

discover. She next took up the story some 2,000 years after Gwevaraugh, during the Middle Ages, when the knowledge was passed on to an order of crusader knights known as the Knights Templar. This mysterious but devoutly religious order of warrior monks used the secrets they possessed to build for themselves not only great mystical power but vast riches and estates throughout Europe.

But all was not well, for the heirs to this knowledge were not without opposition, not only from the physical forces of the envious not so rich and influential, but also from some dark occult power. She did not say what this power was, only that it had one purpose, the destruction of the Templars. This opposition eventually prepared the way for the overthrow of the order, which came to a climax on 13 October, 1307, when the chief Templars were arrested in Paris.

'The task that befell Akhenaten, that befell Gwevaraugh and later the Knights Templar has now been reawakened. This work has now befallen many people, including yourselves.'

'This task, what is it?' said Andy.

'You will know soon, but there is no time to explain it now. There is something you must do, and it must be done quickly.'

Martin and Andy exchanged puzzled glances in the near darkness.

She spoke again, this time more urgently. 'It is no coincidence that it is now October the twelfth. It was on the thirteenth day of October that the Templars were ultimately overthrown. This day holds great significance. Forces could be brought against the Templars on that day, and they were not prepared to meet them. The same forces can be brought against you and others who are to be involved.'

After a short silence she continued.

'The place that the original Egyptian colony was sited, the site of the old hill-fort that I told you of can still be seen. You must go there, and you must be there as the thirteenth day of October begins at midnight. You must be there, all of you.'

'Why? Where is this place?' asked Andy.

'It is called Berry Ring,'

'Where is it? How do we get there?' he said,

Joanna broke in quickly. 'I must go now. You must make haste.'

'One thing before you go,' said Andy hesitantly. 'If the Templars were arrested on the thirteenth of October, and somehow it was meant for us to do this tonight, how did it happen? After all, it was my idea that Graham should try this meditation yesterday and today.'

'Was it?' Joanna replied enigmatically.

'Are you saying I was somehow led to do it?' said Andy.

'Many are led to do things they think coincidental.'

'But where is Berry Ring?' continued Andy, 'You haven't told us.'

Graham inhaled deeply, held his breath for several seconds and then exhaled slowly. After a few minutes silence he moved his arms, turned his head and looked around. Joanna had gone. But this time they had her on tape. Both machines had recorded perfectly.

They found it on the Ordnance Survey map. *Berry Ring*, a roughly oval-shaped hill-fort south-west of the county town of Stafford. Whether Joanna's historical saga was true or not, they would go as she had instructed. There was nothing to lose. Even if nothing happened they would have at least visited an ancient Iron Age hill-fort in the dead of night, an experience in itself.

The silhouette of Stafford castle loomed into view to their right as they drove towards the fort. From its stone ramparts you could see Bery Ring, but only as a clump of dark green trees on a small hill a mile or so distant.

In the light of the headlamps they saw it, a side road to the right signposted *Bury Ring*. A different spelling to the map. (1)

They drove down the narrow country lane, passing occasional old half-timbered houses interspersed with modern bungalows until it became little more than a dirt track. The road came to an end at a cattle grid and a gate bearing the name 'Berry Ring Farm'.

Andy flicked off the lights on his yellow Cortina and cut the engine. He explained that they would be looking for a large

25

circular ditch or ditches. Pre-Roman hill forts were built like that. It could be thirty feet deep and twice as wide, with a diameter of anything up to a few hundred yards.

They stepped out onto the dirt track. It was dark, but not pitch black. The surrounding terrain could be seen in silhouette. In the near distance stood the castle, high and proud on the only hill to be seen thereabouts. In the lowlands next to it shone pinpricks of orange and white light, street lamps in the small towns and villages neighbouring Stafford. A light cloud swept across the sky as the biting wind clawed at their fingers. It was an unusually cold night for early autumn.

Clambering over barbed wire and up a sharp incline they came onto a grassy ridge. By torchlight they followed a winding pathway through the trees, the leaves and dead vegetation rustling against the wind as it brushed through the undergrowth. The ridge sloped away steeply to the right into a deep ditch of about fifteen feet. On the other side it rose even higher.

'This is obviously it,' whispered Andy. He scrabbled down the bank into the ditch as his friends followed. Martin found himself ankle deep in mud and cursed silently. The recent rain had not helped.

Mounting a small incline they reached a spot where the ditch shallowed and became almost even. In the dim light was the circular line of trees delineating the fort, several hundred yards long and about half as wide.

Could Graham's whispering voice be right? Had there really been a warrior queen called Gwevaraugh who fought to defend some long forgotten secret at this very spot? Had it really been a colony of Ancient Egyptians over 3,000 years ago? And if so how could it involve *them* on that cold October night in 1979.

'Twelve o'clock,' announced Andy, squinting at his watch in the darkness. No-one said anything. The wind howled along the gully and through the trees; the cold white stars seemed to move, an illusion of the clouds sweeping across the heavens. Martin peered along the ditch but saw nothing. Graham shook his head in disbelief. Andy gazed skyward.

Something was happening, something unseen but very real. Within themselves they felt it, that indescribable knowing when things are not as they should be. For five minutes they stood in silence, contemplating the bizarre series of events leading to their being in Berry Ring.

Ten minutes later the feeling had passed. Somehow they knew that from that night onwards their lives would never be the same again. What would happen next? What new mysteries would confront them?

'You know something?' said Andy as they reached the car. 'If Gwevaraugh existed and this was her base camp, and she was the historical figure behind the Guinevere legend, do you know what that makes this place?'

'What?' asked Martin.

'Think about it. Guinevere was King Arthur's queen in legend, wasn't she?'

'Yes,' he nodded.

'Well, where did they supposedly live?'

'Camelot.' He replied with a shrug.

'Precisely, Camelot,' he laughed.

On the Sunday afternoon a number of interested parties met at the H.Q. to discuss the situation. Present were Andy, Graham and Martin, Terry Shotton and a friend Alan Beard, a G.P.O. engineer from Alsager in Cheshire. Terry had told Alan of the strange events that had taken place since the conference, and he had expressed interest in what was happening.

Terry and Alan told the others of yet another mysterious event that had occurred that lunchtime. Alan had arrived just after lunch and, as they were talking, the phone rang. It was Penny Blackwill, the medium. She explained how she awoke the previous night, the image of a vivid dream still clear in her mind. She told Terry that she had seen a wide, deep ditch running through some fields, and that this place was somehow of great significance. Penny had given a remarkably accurate description of Berry Ring.

By the early evening they had all agreed that it was certainly more than pure coincidence, that a series of genuine paranormal events were taking place. But this was little comfort. Major questions arose. What *was* going on? Was there some controlling intelligence behind it all, and, if so, what manner of intelligence?

The only chance of a satisfactory answer lay with Graham's whispering voice, Joanna. Did Joanna exist, or was she an unconscious creation of his mind? The first priority was to discover who Joanna really was. Graham had said that he had known several women called Joanna, but he could not see how these could be in any way connected.

They therefore decided to ask help from some the the psychics who had given the messages, starting with Marion. When they telephoned that evening she was baffled. Andy and Graham contacted other psychics; perhaps they could throw light on the affair. Graham called John Ward and Yvonne, using carefully chosen words to avoid influencing future events. Neither could help; nor had they received any psychic impressions about anyone by the name of Joanna.

The only real indication of what was actually behind the events had come from Joanna. According to her they were to be involved in something important, something which began centuries ago with Akhenaten and a secret he possessed, which had been handed down from generation to generation after his followers had travelled to Britain.

So where was the evidence for this? Andy outlined what he had managed to discover from the local library. People, names, dates and places Joanna had spoken of all existed. For hours they discussed the information; none of it contradicted known historical facts, it merely expanded on them and linked hitherto unlinked areas of history together. At least what she had claimed was possible. (See *Appendix P. 197).*

Since no written accounts of this period existed, Andy was unable to discover if there ever was a Gwevaraugh, although Celtic legends did include a certain Queen Gwenhwyfar who later became the Guinevere of the medieval Arthurian romances. The Templars were shrouded in mystery. They came into existence in the early twelfth century A.D. in France, as a full-time military organisation. They were an international body of knights who fought for Christendom in the Holy Land against the Saracens. But the

Knights Templar were more than simply soldiers, they were also monks; Cistercian monks trained to fight as warriors for the Christian church during the Crusades. Over the following two centuries they grew to become a very rich, powerful and influential organisation throughout Europe. Many writers suggest that the Templars studied various forms of occultism or other such esoteric wisdom, most likely taken from the Middle East. They certainly surrounded themselves in mystery, and indeed were eventually excommunicated as heretics by the Roman Catholic Church.

Joanna had told them that the Templars met their end on 13 October, 1307. Andy discovered that this was also correct. They had become unpopular with the French King Philip IV by the early fourteenth century since he evidently owed them a great deal of money. For this reason he decided to destroy them and came to an arrangement with Pope Clement V, who agreed to denounce them and declare them a heretical organisation. With the Pope on his side King Philip arrested the Templars in Paris, including the Grand Master of the Order, Jacques de Moley. They were tried and convicted for heresy and Devil worship. It appeared, however, that the charges were unfounded and simply trumped up by the King and his allies. It was not long before other crowned heads of European countries followed suit, either arresting the Templars or confiscating their lands on the orders of the Pope.

The date King Philip arrested the Templars in Paris was indeed 13 October, 1307. Joanna was right.

Graham knew only a little about the Templars, and was not aware of the importance of 13 October, 1307. (2)

So what were they to make of the Joanna messages? Was her story true? After some discussion they were left with one of two possibilities. Whatever Joanna really was, her story could not be easily dismissed. But was it simply a cleverly constructed tale utilizing unconnected historical facts, or was it really true?

It seemed that the Templars were involved in magical practices, and since the other facts were accurate Joanna's revelation about some dark force having instigated their destruction was perhaps a possibility.

'Maybe the Templars were fighting for what they believed to

29

be the force of good,' said Terry. 'But it may have been that they were using some mystical knowledge to help them in their struggle. Perhaps this is why some opposite force, some evil occult power, was brought against them.'

Everyone stared at him disbelievingly.

'It's only a suggestion, but look at what's been happening,' he said with a shrug. 'Maybe the same could, is about to, happen to us.'

Whatever was about to happen there was only one way to find out. Graham agreed to try to make the Joanna contact again the following evening.

★　★　★　★

On the evening of Monday, 15 October, Graham again fell into the trance state. Once more Joanna's whispering voice spoke through him.

Andy began to ask questions, but they remained unanswered as Joanna explained that she had much to say and that her time was limited. She said that those involved were to undertake a task, a search, a search for something of such importance that they would never believe its full implications.

There existed a force, a power of great evil, she claimed, a power she did not name or attempt to explain. This power had apparently brought about the destruction of many people during the last years of the Megalithic culture in the British Isles, and had existed since that time until today. It had caused much suffering, hardship and grief. What it was, its intended purpose and how it existed she did not explain, saying only that it had manipulated and controlled many people over the ages for its own mysterious purposes. She added that even today it exercised control over people it chose to use.

When the Megalithic peoples passed on their knowledge to Akhenaten they also entrusted to him something that, under certain specific conditions, could be used to ward off this power. Eventually at the right time and in the right hands it could be used to destroy it. This something was a *Green Stone* which she called the *Meonia Stone*. When Akhenaten's followers came to Britain they brought the Meonia Stone with them to the relative safety of their colony in Central England.

This mysterious malific power had sought out the colony and

attempted to destroy them, but Gwevaraugh had defeated those whom it had sent against them and won a temporary victory over the power itself. Soon after this battle the Stone was hidden for safe keeping.

Those who possessed this secret wisdom knew that this dark power would at some future time again attempt to destroy them. Years later certain Knights Templar inherited the secret knowledge and put it to use. Because of this, the evil power eventually moved against them. In 1307, when it finally attempted their destruction, they no longer possessed the Meonia Stone and were overthrown. Only a few survived, continuing as a secret underground movement which later founded a religious body that became known as the Rosicrucians.

Joanna next took up her story in the late sixteenth century, when the Order once more re-located the Stone and decided to use it. Members of this secret organisation had once again tried to establish their headquarters in the centre of England. But some attempted to abuse the secrets they possessed. Because the Stone had at one time been in the possession of the Catholic Mary Queen of Scots, some who held the secrets in the early seventeenth century were Catholics loyal to the Roman Church, and as such were persecuted by the Protestant *régime* of James I. They therefore decided to mount a rebellion. Believing themselves to be invincible they devised a ludicrous scheme to blow up the King and Parliament and then take over the country. This was the Gunpowder Plot of 1605.

Their violent intentions gave this mysterious power the perfect opportunity to destroy them, but still they believed they could overcome it by using the Stone at a certain time, the 31 October. Why this particular date was not explained, except that it was a date long considered to be a time of great mystical power. This power could be harnessed by the Stone and brought to bear against the opposition.

With all prepared for the final day of the plot, those conspirators who were part of the secret organisation tried to use the Stone. They failed. In becoming men of violence they had lost what they once possessed, the power to defeat evil. Still they elected to continue with the plot, but on 5 November Guy Fawkes was discovered beneath the Houses of Parliament and arrested.

By that evening all that remained of the proposed rebellion were forty or so conspirators fleeing from the Sheriff of Worcester's men across the Worcestershire countryside. Amongst them were some of those who were members of the secret society. Most, however, knew nothing of this society and had justified their actions only out of loyalty to the Catholic cause. Of those who *were* members, Thomas Wyntour and Robert Catesby were the chief conspirators.

That day the fleeing plotters stayed overnight at the Worcestershire home of Robert Wyntour, Thomas Wyntour's brother and co-conspirator. It was there at Huddington Court that Catesby, seeing that all was lost, handed the Stone to Robert Wyntour's wife Gertrude Wyntour who he charged with its safe keeping while they tried to make their escape.

The conspirators left Huddington next morning, and by the evening had made their way to Holbeach House. Here they were surrounded by the Sheriff's men and either killed or arrested. Gertrude Wyntour had made sure the stone was safely hidden and it was never retrieved.

Joanna said that people in various parts of the country had been chosen to perform a task, and whether they like it or not *Parasearch* were involved. For this reason the power of the opposition would move against them. If their task was to succeed they must rediscover the Stone by 31 October.

Joanna said she did not know where the Stone was hidden, but she did say that someone else had been involved with Gertrude Wyntour, a close friend named Humphrey Pakington, who had lived at a nearby manor called Harvington Hall.

The Stone could be found if they could crack a secret code, from which its whereabouts could be logically deduced. The only clue she gave was that Humphrey Pakington had commissioned a series of paintings on the walls of Harvington Hall that might hold the key to the puzzle. She said these pictures were called the *Nine Worthies*.

She went on to make an even more startling revelation. The opposition they could expect involved living people who would also be searching for the Stone.

Joanna concluded by explaining that she could not talk to them again until the Stone was found. It would be too dangerous. The opposition might have the power to intercept all communication.

★ ★ ★ ★

In the space of a few short months *Parasearch* had been thrown headlong into a bizarre tale of Ancient Egyptians, a Celtic queen and Medieval warrior monks. On the instructions of a strange whispering voice they had travelled to an ancient hill-fort to prepare their minds for a coming task, a task to oppose a mysterious occult power and to rediscover something called the Meonia Stone buried centuries ago after the ill-fated Gunpowder Plot of 1605.

Never had there been so fantastic a story! To ignore it would be irresponsible. However incredible, however impossible, it *might* be true. Their investigations had to continue. If the Meonia Stone existed then they must find it.

But first they must check the facts. Did Humphrey Pakington, Harvington Hall and the Nine Worthies exist? For that matter how much of this subsequent Joanna information was correct?

Chapter Five

———◆———

The Nine Worthies

ANDY spent Tuesday at the local reference library checking the facts. Was there more to the Gunpowder Plot than history had so far revealed, and did a mysterious green jewel called the Meonia Stone really exist?

Once again the accuracy of Joanna's story was astounding. He found confirmation that the Gunpowder Plot had been initiated by a number of Catholic extremists persecuted under the reign of James I. The plot had been the brainchild of Robert Catesby, a country squire from Ashby St. Ledgers in Northamptonshire. Catesby had convinced a number of close friends that his plan to blow up the King and his ministers at the state opening of Parliament was feasible, and eventually a storage cellar was rented beneath the House of Lords. Barrel loads of gunpowder were smuggled in and conspirator Guy Fawkes volunteered to remain behind and light the fuses, then make good his escape at the last possible moment. But the plan went disastrously wrong. On the night before the opening of Parliament on 5 November,1605 the King's soldiers broke in, discovered the gunpowder and arrested Fawkes.

Realising that the plot was discovered, Catesby and the other chief conspirators attempted to rouse a rebellion among the Catholics of the Midland counties, but met with no support.

This group, comprising forty or so conspirators, were thus left to fend for themselves and escape the authorities. As Joanna had said they spent the night of Wednesday, 6 November at Huddington Court, the home of Robert Wyntour, but nowhere was there any mention of a Stone, or in fact anything being handed to Gertrude Wyntour for safe keeping. However, if Catesby really had possessed this Green Stone, which perhaps acted as a symbol of unity for their cause, then Gertrude would have been the most likely person to have been entrusted with it. She had remained behind when the plotters moved on after their overnight stay at Huddington, and so was perhaps the last trusted person, not directly implicated in the plot, that they had contact with before being intercepted.

In the early hours of the seventh the conspirators left Huddington to make for North Wales, where they hoped to receive assistance. But the weather was against them and the unruly band did not get far. The heaviest rainfall for years made the muddy roads virtually impassable. Catesby and his followers must certainly have known that their chances were slim indeed. So if they had possessed this mysterious Stone, which they wished to safeguard from enemy hands, then Huddington was possibly their last chance for securing its safety. The following day their worst fears were realised when they made a last stand against the Sheriff of Worcester's soldiers at Holbeach House, the home of sympathiser Stephen Lyttleton, some twenty five miles away. After a brief but desperate struggle, Catesby and a number of his fellows were killed, the remaining conspirators being arrested and swiftly taken to the Tower of London. (1)

Andy went on to explain what he had discovered about Harvington Hall, and the man who had shared the secret of the Meonia Stone, Humphrey Pakington.

Once again Joanna's information had proved correct. Harvington Hall had existed at the time of the Gunpowder Plot and, as she had claimed, it still stood today.

Not only had Pakington existed, but it was he who was chiefly responsible for the building of the present house. Although Andy had found no direct correlation between the Gunpowder Plot and Pakington, there was little doubt that the Pakington family had been Roman Catholics, since the old hall was riddled with secret places built during the sixteenth and seventeenth centuries to hide Jesuit priests whose capture would have meant death. Even the pictures Joanna had described could still be seen at Harvington and, as she had said, were called 'The Nine Worthies'. These old paintings depicted nine heroic characters from history and legend, but who they represented or who had had them commissioned he had been unable to discover.

Then an intriguing question arose. If Joanna knew about a coded message, how was it that she was unable to say where the Stone was hidden? Eventually they decided that there was little hope of answering that particular question until they could discover who Joanna actually was.

Andy was uncertain if there was more to the Gunpowder Plot than a simple Catholic rebellion, or whether it had links with this secret mystical organisation dating back to the Knights Templar and Akhenaten in Egypt. They would have to consult historians or spend a great deal more time researching before they could resolve these questions.

So were the Rosicrucians connected with the Gunpowder Plot as Joanna had said? Here there was a problem. The Rosicrucians seemed to have been Protestants, or at least anti-Catholic. However, few historical events are so veiled in mystery. Perhaps there was a link; indeed many historians admit that it is very probable that they will never know the real truth about the Plot.

But what about the Rosicrucians themselves? The name Rosicrucian came from the title *Fraternity of the Rose Cross*, the name derived from the symbol of the Order, a red rose mounted at the centre of a Calvary cross. In all the more objectively researched books that Andy had consulted, the authors admitted that it was impossible to say anything with certainty about the Rosicrucians, since from its very outset the organisation had been shrouded in mystery.

The Rosicrucians first made themselves known to the world at Kassel in Germany in 1614, when a mysterious document was publicly circulated. The manuscript known as the *Fama* declared to the world the existence of an international brotherhood called the Order of the Rose Cross, whose purpose it was to bring about a new age of enlightenment. They claimed to possess hitherto undisclosed mystical knowledge which they would impart to the new brothers they hoped to attract, and urged the like minded among the intelligentsia of Europe to join them. The only problem for anyone wishing to join them was that they left no forwarding address, while the author or authors of this document remained an enigma. (2)

The following year a second Rosicrucian document appeared in

Kassel, and once again the anonymous author urged the same response. (3) The third and final document in the series was published in Strasbourg in 1616. (4) These three documents, which came to be known as the Rosicrucian Manifestos, were for the most part allegorical or coded messages and full of alchemical and occult symbolism, although their real purpose has never been fully understood.

However, most authorities agree that the intention of the authors of the Manifestos was to make themselves known, and to excite the academic world into learning more about this anonymous and secret Brotherhood in order, at some later date, to introduce themselves to certain chosen scholars. The later history of the Rosicrucians is unclear. Only one thing appears certain, and this is that the Manifestos were undeniably anti-Catholic, since the enlightenment they were advocating, namely free thinking in religion, the arts and the sciences, could only be achieved under a Protestant *régime*. Indeed, the occult and mystical flavour of the symbolism in the Manifestos would have been considered heretical by the seventeenth century Roman Catholic Church.

In the later years of the seventeenth century, and, indeed, until the present day, many and varied mystical, occult or religious groups have appeared, all claiming to be true Rosicrucians. Yet most historians agree that there is little evidence to link these organisations with the authors of the original Manifestos. (5)

In addition to the accuracy of Joanna's information concerning the Gunpowder Plot, something happened which indicated that she may well have been right about the possible links between the Knights Templar and the Rosicrucians. Only a few weeks later the BBC broadcast a programme in its 'Chronicle' series entitled 'The Shadow of the Templars'. In this documentary writer and broadcaster Henry Lincoln suggested that the Rosicrucians were heirs to the lost wealth of the Templars. When the Order was outlawed vast amounts of their wealth disappeared and was never found. Lincoln advocated that the Rosicrucians were eventually founded using this money, as a secret underground group to carry on where the Templars left off.

★　★　★　★

That evening Alan Beard telephoned the Wolverhampton flat to explain how he had been lying in bed, half awake and half asleep, in the early hours of that morning, when a vivid image suddenly flashed into his mind and he found himself looking at what he felt was Berry Ring. In the sky above the centre of the ring he saw an egg-shaped object glowing white, which gradually changed into a small green stone. He next saw the stone set in an old pewter ring.

Andy and Graham were taken aback by Alan's description. He could give no further details, except to say that he felt very strongly that this vision was connected with the events they had been discussing on Sunday. In describing the stone he said it was oval-shaped, about an inch long and green in colour. The green was similar to jade. He later gave them a drawing of the ring and the stone.

The most amazing thing about Alan's dream was that he knew nothing about the events of Monday evening, and hence nothing about Joanna's description of a green stone, the supposed Meonia Stone. His vision was independent confirmation of the latest Joanna information, and firm enough to justify further investigation. The question, however, was where to begin? It was decided that the best place would be Harvington Hall, since it was here, in the paintings of the Nine Worthies, that Joanna said there was a secret coded message.

So began the search for the Meonia Stone, and with it a quest that would lead those involved into a head-on clash with forces beyond their comprehension.

Just three miles south-east of Kidderminster in the heart of Worcestershire, a winding lane leaves the A448, giving visitors their first glimpse of Harvington Hall. A jumble of roofs and red-brick walls encompassed by a deep moat, this splendid Elizabethan manor house remains almost unchanged from the days of the Gunpowder Plot. Some parts have been renovated, but for the most it stands unaltered since those eventful years of the early seventeenth century.

In the 1920's the Hall was little more than an ivy-covered ruin, its moat choked with vegetation. In 1923 it was bought and given to the

Roman Catholic Archdiocese of Birmingham and, in 1929 Arch-bishop Thomas Williams took steps to safeguard it from falling into irreparable decay.

A stone bridge leads across the moat into the cobbled courtyard. Walking across it that warm afternoon they could not help but wonder if Humphrey Pakington was really involved in some strange mystical sect. Had he truly played a part in a mysterious cosmic game of chess in which they had now become inextricably involved?

As they entered the large oak-panelled room called the Withdraw-ing Room, the afternoon sun came in through the leaded windows, casting long shadows on the antique furnishings. On the wall beside the window hung three paintings. One was of a man, middle aged with receding hair and a pointed beard: Humphrey Pakington. According to the guidebook he was born in 1555 and died in 1631. So it seemed that he had survived the reprisals dealt out to the Catholics following their abortive conspiracy.

The labyrinth of narrow but well-lit passageways led from room to room in the old building. Here and there were secret places, hide holes for the Jesuit priests. Heavy wooden panels that slid away in the walls, hidden trap doors beneath floorboards, and staircases that lifted to reveal small claustrophobic rooms. In these cold, dank holes, the renegade priests must have hidden, sometimes for days on end, as the house was searched from top to bottom by agents of the Protestant authorities.

The Nine Worthies were not as they had expected, paintings on canvas, but mural decorations on the wall of a narrow passage on the second floor. Although faded with age, portions remained of six. The Nine Worthies were evidently a favourite subject of illustration in the sixteenth and seventeenth centuries. They depicted nine heroes from history, myth and legend, all renowned for heroic deeds, Judas Maccabaeus, David, Joshua, Julius Caesar, Alexander, Hector, Charlemagne, Arthur and Godfrey de Bouillon. Sometimes they would include Hercules, Pompey, or Guy of Warwick.

The six remaining murals at Harvington represent the biblical Joshua, in armour, carrying a lance and seated on a horse. Samson, as a long-haired bearded figure holding above his head the jaw bone of an ass, with which, the Old Testament tells us, he slew the Philis-tines. Hercules, hero of Greek mythology. Pompey, the Roman general. Guy of Warwick, champion of the Saxon King Athelstan.

Lastly, a young man wielding a huge broad sword, that some believe to be King David.

The only way to crack the supposed code, accepting that Joanna was right, was to assume that Pakington had left the message for the Rosicrucians. But here was a dilemma. Why, if the Stone existed, had the Rosicrucians not retrieved it? It seemed likely that only a handful of people in England knew about the Stone, and most of these had been either killed or arrested. Perhaps of those who knew of this sacred relic, only Pakington or Gertrude Wyntour had remained alive. So why had Pakington not smuggled a message out of the country to the Rosicrucians in Germany? As a Catholic he was watched closely after the plot, and probably had the Worthies painted to reveal the location of the Stone in the event of his death.

If, therefore, the murals had been painted for the benefit of the Rosicrucians, and concealed a coded message, then they could expect to find some form of symbolism that would have been recognised by the Rosicrucians. The known Rosicrucian documents of the early seventeenth century had used occult, alchemical and astrological symbolism, so possibly somewhere in the paintings evidence of this would be uncovered.

It was the number nine, the *Nine* Worthies, that first intimated the possibility of Rosicrucian symbolism being employed. Of course, it may have had no connection with the Nine Worthies, but nonetheless it was something Pakington might have utilized.

Joanna had of course spoken of *The Nine*. In occult and mystical tradition *The Nine* continually appear. For centuries there has existed a mystical legend and tradition that somewhere in the world there are nine grand spiritual masters who control man's ultimate destiny. They are known as 'The Nine Unknown Men.' In Rosicrucian tradition the Inner Order of the Rose Cross comprises nine spritual overseers, The nine 'Secret Chiefs', sometimes called the 'Illuminati' of simply 'The Nine.' Was this some form of indication to the Rosicrucians, who would undoubtedly have known and used such symbolism? (6)

Next there was the figure of David slaying Goliath. But David had slain Goliath with a sling, not a huge broad sword as depicted. Samson was accurately shown wielding a jaw bone, so it seemed unlikely that the artist would have portrayed David with a long sword. Since one of the main Nine Worthies usually depicted was

King Arthur, it was concluded that the figure was more likely to be him than David. Arthur, as a young man, wielding Excalibur as related in the Arthurian legend.

As Graham examined the Arthur figure he first noticed something strange about the position of the sword above his head.

They scrutinised the paintings closely, hoping to find some occult or mystical design, and perhaps an astrological symbol. But there was nothing so obvious or simple.

Graham looked again at Arthur wielding the broad sword, and then at the other figures and the way in which they held their respective weapons.

'I don't suppose it means anything,' he said, 'but notice the way they're holding their weapons. Above their heads in the same position.'

The Joshua figure on horseback held a long lance to his side, but the other figures held their swords, or, in Samson's case, the jawbone, above their heads in an awkward horizontal position.

'That's the only thing that strikes me an unusual about the pictures,' continued Graham. 'They are all holding their weapons in the same way.'

Andy studied the paintings and nodded in agreement. 'You're right,' he said, 'it does seem odd. And I can't help thinking I've seen that somewhere before.'

Graham then suggested that they discover who it was that had commissioned the paintings. Was it really Humphrey Pakington as Joanna had claimed?

'Let's ask the guide,' said Andy.

The Pakington family had owned Harvington since 1529 when the property was bought by John Pakington, a rich lawyer much favoured by Henry VIII. But the first reference to the family living in the Hall is in a letter dated January 1582-83, when Humphrey Pakington had taken up residence and begun the rebuilding.

The Pakingtons were one of the many Worcestershire families who refused to give their allegiance to the Protestant Church during the reign of Elizabeth I, and had remained loyal to the Catholic Church.

In the reign of Elizabeth I, severe punishments were given in an attempt to suppress the Roman Catholic religion. Every priest was ordered to quit the kingdom on pain of death. The penalty for saying

Mass included life imprisonment; to help or harbour a priest was a felony and as such punishable by hanging. Every Catholic was ordered to attend the Protestant parish church on Sunday, or incur heavy fines if they refused. Those who did not attend were known as Recusants. Humphrey Pakington was one such Recusant.

And how about Humphrey Pakington and the Gunpowder Plot? Evidently he had not been implicated, although he had spent many years confined to Harvington following the conspiracy. But this had been a general policy for many Catholic gentry.

So was this a possible explanation for the coded message, assuming it existed? If Pakington had been confined to Harvington, then he would have been unable to take the Stone out of the country. But perhaps there was no-one else he felt he could trust. If, after all, the Stone was what Joanna had claimed, then his reluctance was understandable.

On the other hand he was more than likely being watched at every turn, and any messages would have been immediately intercepted.

When questioned about Pakington's later life, the guide explained that he had spent some years under house arrest, and when eventually released had travelled to France, staying there for some years before returning to Harvingon where he died in 1631.

Who had commissioned the painting of the Nine Worthies no-one knew for sure, but it is certain to have been during Pakington's time at the Hall.

One particularly interesting point that the guide did mention concerning the Worthies, were the exceptional circumstances that had allowed the paintings to survive for so long. It seemed that in or about the year 1660, Pakington's daughter Lady Mary Yate had the paintings whitewashed over. Why she should have done this is something of a mystery.

If the Stone existed and Pakington had played his part as Joanna had claimed, then why was it never recovered? The most likely answer was that Pakington had not been a figure of major importance in the mystical society which Joanna had referred to, namely the Rosicrucians. Obviously he knew quite a lot, including the Rosicrucian involvement, but perhaps not enough to know who the Rosicrucian fraternity really were. Otherwise he would have informed them of the whereabouts of the Stone upon his release from custody. This seemed pretty certain.

Perhaps Pakington had been given the names of Rosicrucian members in 1605, but by the time of his release from house arrest during the 1620s it was possible that they were no longer living, or he was unable to locate them. Possibly his time in France was spent trying to make contact with the Rosicrucians.

So it seemed likely that Pakington was merely an accessory called upon to help by Gertrude Wyntour, and perhaps the only person she could trust at a time when she herself was in grave peril.

Andy and Graham left Harvington with more than enough to continue the search. As each new piece of evidence emerged the Joanna story became more and more likely, not least the information regarding the white-washing of the Nine Worthies. If Pakington's daughter knew of the importance of the paintings, she may well have attempted to preserve them as best she could.

'The important thing is to understand Humphrey Pakington,' said Andy, as they drove away from Harvington. 'Get to know his lifestyle, his movements, his friends, his situation. The more we know about Pakington, the more chance we have of beginning to think Pakington Logic.'

'Pakington Logic?' Graham repeated.

'Yes. Put ourselves in his shoes. Think what we would have done in his situation. Decide where we would have hidden the Stone.'

'So where do we go from here?'

'Well, we know what happened to Pakington after the Gunpowder Plot, so let's see what we can find out about Gertrude Wyntour.'

The next stage in the search would therefore have to be Huddington Court, which still stands today. Unlike Harvington, however, Huddington is now a private residence tucked away in the Worcestershire countryside.

The Gunpowder Plot had ended, as Joanna had described, with the last parting of the small band of conspirators from Huddington Court. All the persons mentioned in the trance account had also existed, but so far nothing had been discovered about the Green Stone. Neither had Andy's enquiries shed light on the mysterious Gertrude Wyntour, wife of conspirator Robert Wyntour, the country squire of Huddington. Following the ill-fated parting of her husband and the others there was a blank. What had befallen her?

Chapter Six

———————•———————

Pakington Logic

ABOUT ten miles south-east of Harvington is the old Tudor court of Huddington, standing a little way back from a quiet country lane. The tiny hamlet of Huddington consists of only a few farm buildings and the occasional tithe cottage.

On the old iron gates was the well-weathered sign, 'Huddington Court'. The gates were jammed open by the long grass and undergrowth that encroached upon the narrow driveway between the tall unkempt hedgerows on either side. From the road the court itself could not be seen. The trees that surrounded it were still well foliated with unfallen leaves. Could this centuries old building hold a long-forgotten secret? Was there some local legend, some seldom narrated country tale of hidden treasure? A precious green gemstone hidden somewhere in the house? A priceless jewel that many had tried to find?

Leaving the car to obtain a better view, they could make out a tall decorated chimney pot, like a finger pointing in accusation at the sky, standing alone above the thick foliage. The smell of the Autumn air, the soft breeze rustling through the trees and blowing the occasional falling leaf against the car. The atmosphere was one of romantic adventure, a sense of impending excitement and perhaps fulfilment.

'Who lives here?' Graham asked.

Andy shrugged 'Joanna perhaps,' he said, with a smile.

And they both laughed.

Following the driveway, the old manor slowly revealed itself. First

47

the tall Elizabethan chimneys, then the uneven roof and the black timbers contrasting against the white walls. From without Huddington Court appeared almost as it must have looked to the ill-fated Gunpowder conspirators.

The manor was neatly painted and the leaded bay windows unbroken. The pathway led to a second set of iron gates, and a full view of the court.

'The last known whereabouts of the Meonia Stone,' said Andy, leaning over the gate.

The wide driveway leading some thirty or forty yards from them towards the house was well kept, as was the neatly cut lawn which led to a little wall ornamented with Grecian urns.

As they gazed towards the old manor with its majestic gables, they could not help but picture that ill-fated day almost four centuries ago. Before dawn on a cold November morning, the dispirited band of conspirators had mounted their horses. Although frightened, some were still prepared to die for their faith, while others no longer cared. All were aware that their attempted flight to safety stood little chance of success. It must have been a moving sight. Robert Wyntour, who surely knew little of Catesby's crazy intentions, embraced his wife and children for the last time. As he joined his comrades on the journey that would eventually lead him to the gallows, he no doubt gazed back to see Gertrude standing bravely, forcing back her tears. Perhaps Robert Catesby, the chief conspirator, also halted his mount at the gateway for a last look at Gertrude clasping the precious gemstone he had entrusted to her. The sacred relic that had meant so much to so many for so long, passed on for centuries to vanish for ever from that mysterious sect as Catesby turned his horse and rode away into the early morning mists. Now, three hundred and seventy four years later, two young men had arrived at the same gateway, prompted by some unimaginable force to return and reclaim the Meonia Stone.

The place looked deserted as they rang the doorbell. At first there was no answer. They rang again. An elderly lady leant out of one of the ground-floor windows. Andy told her they were researching for a magazine feature.

'We're investigating a local historical mystery about the Gunpowder Plot. Can we speak with the present owner of the house?'

They were not the first people inquiring into the history of Huddington Court. The woman said that the owner was in the garden, and would be pleased to help them if possible. They made their way into the grounds behind the house, following the narrow path, flanked by privet hedges and rhododendron bushes, and crossed a stone bridge spanning the slow-moving stream that wound its way past the house towards the River Avon. On the other side of the stream the garden became a little wilder, an old sundial, statuettes and a summer house. They had almost given up hope of locating anyone in the maze of gravel covered pathways, when, as if from nowhere, an elderly gentleman appeared.

Andy quickly told his story and their belief that a jewel or stone might have been hidden after the Gunpowder Plot.

The old man had never heard of any such legend, although he knew about the events of the plot concerning his house. However, he did know something about Gertrude Wyntour.

Gertrude had not been implicated in the plot, and the authorities had been satisfied that she was ignorant of her husband's and brother-in-law's activities. Her younger brother-in-law John Wyntour had been condemned to death, for no other reason than because he was their brother. Like Pakington, Gertrude was confined to house arrest and spent the rest of her life at Huddington.

They asked him about the later life of Gertrude Wyntour. Had she perhaps left anything behind, a portrait maybe, or something she had made or commissioned? Yes, she had, replied the old man. A set of Mass vestments on which she had spent much of her time during her imprisonment at Huddington. Could these possibly hold some sort of clue? Unlikely, but worth a try. They were now at the Roman Catholic chapel at Kemerton in Gloucestershire.

Before they left the owner told them that one of the windows, the east window of the old dining hall, is still called 'Lady Wyntour's Window.' Tradition says that from there she watched for her husband's return. And more. Her ghost had been seen on a number of occasions. The spectral apparition of a dark-clad woman gazing forlornly from the window.

As they drove away from Huddington they looked up at the

window, half expecting Lady Wyntour's ghost to manifest and help them solve the mystery.

As the days passed, many hours were spent researching the tumultuous years of history surrounding the Gunpowder Plot, but nowhere was there evidence or record of the illusive Green Stone.

Graham spent many hours poring over the pictures of the Nine Worthies, while Andy telephoned or visited different experts known to them through *Parasearch*. Authorities on the occult and Rosicrucian history were consulted but nothing new emerged. Phone calls to the psychics who had forwarded the messages over the weeks also proved fruitless.

When Terry Shotton arrived at the headquarters that Thursday evening, 18 October, he found the front room office littered with maps, charts and open books.

Andy had tried another line of inquiry. Had anyone else, apart from Pakington and Gertrude, known the secret and imparted information about the location of the Stone? What about the surviving conspirators rounded up at Holbeach? Perhaps they had attempted to send word in code of its hiding place during their interrogations. These statements would have been read aloud at the trials. But once again this drew a blank, apart from the mention by Thomas Wyntour, extracted under torture in the Tower of London, that before his death Catesby had 'took from his neck a cross of gold which he always used to wear about him.' Had Catesby once worn the Stone in the cross around his neck? (1)

Terry had felt that Alan Beard's vision of the Stone and Berry Ring was significant, and he decided to visit the old fort to see for himself. He reasoned that perhaps the Stone was hidden at Berry Ring. Indeed, three of them had already been instructed to go there by Joanna at midnight on 12 October, and Alan's vision had linked the Stone and the ancient fort. Maybe he would receive some psychic impression.

As he stood alone in the cattle field that is now the central plateau of the ring, he felt something indescribable, a feeling that somehow it had all happened before, that same indistinct but nevertheless real sense that the others had felt when, at dead of night, they too had journeyed there.

Terry decided to visit the medium, Penny Blackwill, to see if she had had another psychic impression that could help. She had not.

Nor could Alan Beard help further. Terry then felt that it might be a good idea to sweep Berry Ring with a metal detector; if the Stone was set in a pewter ring then a detector would find it. However, because of the time involved, he decided to await further developments that might positively indicate that Berry Ring was the correct site.

As the three of them sat talking late into the evening they felt a sense of urgency. But why? If the Stone had lain hidden for nearly four centuries then it could surely wait a little longer. Or could it? Joanna had said that it must be found by 31 October, because others were also searching for it. Perhaps it was only Joanna's words which gave them this sense of urgency. Or was there perhaps something more?

'Why the hell should the thirty first of October be important?' asked Terry.

'It's Halloween,' said Andy, half seriously.

'The night of witches.' joked Terry.

'Exactly,' said Andy. 'I don't think we should underestimate the wisdom of the ancients, who believed that magical powers could be invoked on Halloween.' (2)

Was Joanna thus implying that on this day the Stone could call upon these primeval forces? And was there really some opposite group also seeking the Stone? These questions would have to wait, now they must concentrate on their search. What should be their next step?

They decided that their best hope of solving the riddle was to put themselves into Pakington's and Gertrude Wyntour's situation.

It seemed certain that Pakington had only become involved unwittingly, and the same probably applied to Gertrude. Both knew to whom they had to take the Stone, but as Catholics closely associated with the conspirators they were arrested. They had little time to act. So had there been a pre-arranged hiding place for the Stone agreed with the Rosicrucians? Probably not, for the plot had backfired at the last moment.

It was probable that Catesby had instructed Gertrude Wyntour to take the Stone to a specific person, but the urgency of the situation had prevented this. She had therefore sought the aid of her close friend and fellow Catholic Humphrey Pakington.

Perhaps a messenger had arrived at Harvington Hall and told

51

Pakington to make haste to Huddington. There Gertrude and Pakington devised a plan to hide the Stone. But if this was so, why had they not despatched a messenger to the Rosicrucian contact? Most likely they could find no trustworthy person. The discovery of the Catholic plot would have cast suspicion on the employees as government informers, and even if they were not they knew they were likely to suffer interrogation. The threat of the rack and other tortures would be sufficient to make them bargain for their freedom in order to prove their loyalty to the crown. What better hope for clemency than to deliver a secret message into the hands of the government? What could Gertrude and Pakington do in such fearful circumstances?

'We must think Pakington logic,' Andy repeated.

Where would *they* decide to hide the Stone? In some place that the Rosicrucians would be able to find, assuming they knew enough to understand the symbolism and traditions.

At the time of hiding the Stone, Pakington would not know he would live to leave a permanent message. That came later. The Stone's hiding place needed to be obvious to their Rosicrucian colleagues.

'But they did live,' protested Terry, 'and they may have moved it from its original place when they had more time.'

'I disagree,' said Andy. 'I believe they couldn't risk collecting it because they were being watched. They were also prevented from getting a message or the Stone itself out.'

'Unless it was in the house somewhere,' said Terry.

'Again too much of a risk. They might have been searched.'

So where could Pakington and Gertrude have hidden the Stone? Did they believe that any hiding place would have to remain undiscovered for many years? If so, this would have influenced their choice.

What were the possibilities? Where would they have hidden the Stone? In an old building, beneath a statue, a wayside cross, in a tomb or vault, or merely buried it in the ground?

They tried to imagine, as Pakington must have done, a Rosicrucian messenger arriving one day in the future in search of the Meonia Stone. What had happened to it? Surely their comrades must have deposited it somewhere where it could be found.

After some time they discussed an interesting possibility: a place name. A place that would remain unaltered. Perhaps a natural landmark with a meaningful name association.

Surely the Nine Worthies could give them the clue they were looking for.

Figure of Samson holding jawbone in the St George Parry at Harvington Hall. From the Nine Worthies.

Chapter Seven

———————◆———————

The St. George Parry

REASONING that the hiding place was likely to be somewhere relatively close to Harvington and Huddington, they consulted a map of Worcestershire. Was there a place name that was in some way linked with the Nine Worthies? They could find nothing that seemed possible.

One of the names of the Worthies represented at Harvington maybe? Samson, Joshua, Arthur, Guy of Warwick. Could it be Warwick? It seemed doubtful. No, it had to be something more significant.

'I think it could be Berry Ring,' said Terry. 'If the Stone was set in a ring as Alan said then they may have buried it there.'

They stared at Terry. 'It's logical, isn't it? Especially if Berry Ring's importance was known to them and the Rosicrucians. I know it might sound crazy but it's what I'd do.'

It was a possibility. A pun on words. Joanna had told them to go to Berry Ring, and Penny and Alan Beard had both seen it in visions. In Alan's vision the ring was directly connected with the Stone. But Berry Ring is over forty miles from the central Worcestershire area, a long distance to travel in those bygone days.

'I think we're looking for something a bit nearer to where they lived' said Andy. 'Especially if they had to hide it in a hurry. I don't think they'd have gone that far. It's also unlikely they'd have known about Berry Ring.'

Of course it all depended on whether or not the Stone was where they had originally hidden it or whether it had been moved at some later date. If the former then it would undoubtedly be near Harvington or Huddington.

Their best chance would be to split forces. Terry would try Berry Ring, perhaps taking Alan Beard with him in case he received further impressions. They could also use a metal detector, or even enlist the help of a dowser. Graham and Andy meanwhile would follow the Worcestershire trail. They also decided to work from old maps rather than the modern Ordnance Survey ones.

Before Terry left he made an observation. 'Perhaps,' he said, the Stone has already been found, recovered by the Rosicrucians years ago.'

'If that were so Joanna wouldn't have us looking for it,' said Andy.

The following day, Friday 19 October, nothing new had been discovered, and so they decided to test the possibility that Gertrude Wyntour's hand-made vestments might hold some clue.

That day, with Alan Beard and Terry Shotton they travelled to Kemerton. Speaking with an old priest in the presbytery he told them of their wasted journey. The ancient, beautifully embroidered vestments were indeed there, and they had been made by Lady Wyntour of Huddington, but not Gertrude Wyntour. The Lady was Mary Wyntour, a member of the Wyntour family in the latter half of the seventeenth century.

When he heard of their interest in Catholic history, he showed them some very old stained-glass windows in his chapel. The Catholic church was, of course, a modern nineteenth century building, but in the porch were two small stained-glass windows which were many centuries older.

As they studied one of the windows they were suddenly reminded of the Harvington Hall Worthies. The window depicted St. George slaying the dragon, but it was the way in which he held his sword that caught their attention. Like the Nine Worthies St. George wielded his sword near horizontally above his head. What was the meaning of this unusual stance? The priest did not know.

That evening Andy again phoned various authorities on the occult to ask their advice. Did it mean anything to the Rosicrucians? And eventually he found an answer. Whether the Rosicrucians would have known of it or not, the position meant something in the traditional art of sword fencing. For centuries it had been called The St. George Parry, the sword-held position associated in chivalry with St. George the dragon slayer.(1)

In myth St. George slew the dragon, but in Christian and occult tradition it has two different meanings. In the former it represents the ultimate power to overcome evil, the dragon being the power of evil, the Devil. But in occult tradition it represents the exact opposite, the path to mystical power. In pre-Christian pagan tradition, the dragon or serpent represents the higher spiritual forces of nature. The myth of slaying the dragon is to gain mastery over these forces. When the Christian church superceded the pagans, the Christian authorities considered the pagan beliefs improper, and hence the dragon or serpent power became the work of the Devil. (2)

The pre-Christian pagan Celtic peoples believed that there were places where the serpent power, the mystical power of nature, could be tapped or evoked. Centres of spiritual energy, the places of the dragon. When the Christians took over and attempted to suppress the old faith and win over the people, they often sited their early churches and chapels on ground already sacred to the old religion. The most important of these sites were the places of the serpent power, and the simple churches were later replaced by the more impressive medieval Gothic churches. Thus many churches still standing today are built on these old dragon sites. To display the power of the church over that of the dragon faith, the churches were often dedicated to the Christian dragon-slaying saints, namely St. George, and St. Michael.

Examples include the old tower — all that remains — of St. Michael's church on Glastonbury Tor, long known to have been a pre-Christian sacred site. Brentor on Dartmoor in Devon, where St. Michael's church stands out high above the surrounding moorland. The old church is surrounded by the remains of an even older pre-Roman earthwork. The 13th century parish church of Thriplow in Cambridgeshire dedicated to St. George is yet another example, for it stands on an ancient mound sacred to the pre-Christian religion.

So here they had a two-fold meaning. The slaying of the dragon, a great power over evil, and a power to harness the highest spiritual forces of nature. They were looking for the Meonia Stone which, according to Joanna, had the power to overcome some great evil, in addition to other undisclosed powers. Presumably those who hid it knew or believed it to be so.

So could the St. George Parry position therefore be referring to the Stone, the serpent power of the Celts? Joanna had said that the secret of the Stone had been passed on through the heart of the British Celtic religion. It was all beginning to fit. Could this be what the Nine Worthies were saying? Were they really alluding to the Stone?

But there was still something else. St. George holds much the same significance as the legendary King Arthur, who symbolises all that oppose evil. Arthur is symbolic of the force of the land, in other words the dragon force personified. Once again they had a Celtic link. Guinevere in Arthurian legend was the Celtic Gwenhwyfar, but did the Rosicrucians know this? Certainly one of the Pakington Worthy figures represented King Arthur.

Had they begun to crack the Pakington code? If so, where should they look next? What else was Pakington trying to tell them?

A St. George's Church perhaps? But where? Surely he would never have risked such proximity to the authorities. But maybe he did, choosing the least expected place.

Shortly after Terry and Alan left, Marion Sunderland phoned and spoke to Graham. She had been sitting at home watching television when a strong impression had suddenly flashed into her mind. She saw a sword, lying on a stone slab at the bottom of some water, and there was something else, a smell, a very unpleasant smell of rotting vegetation. Interesting, since she knew nothing of the St. George Parry discoveries. Could this mean anything? A sword under water. Immediately, one thing came to mind. King Arthur's Excalibur, which was represented in the Nine Worthies. Excalibur, a sword above the head, the St. George Parry position. St. George synonymous with King Arthur, Celtic legends and Guinevere. This must be it!

'Excalibur!' Graham cried. 'The St. George Parry position. What does it remind you of?' He held a ruler above his head in an assumed stance. Andy shook his head.

'In the King Arthur legend what happened to Excalibur?'

'It was thrown by Sir Bedivere into the lake.'

'And?'

'An arm came out of the lake and caught it,' said Andy.

'Exactly,' Graham exclaimed, 'like this,' thrusting his hand overhead in the St. George Parry position.

'My God,' said Andy, 'you're right!'

Excalibur is also representative of the force wielded by Arthur. A magic sword to overcome evil, the same as the Meonia Stone. So what was this telling them? They had already decided approximately where Pakington might have hidden the Stone, not too far from either Harvington or Huddington, and that it would certainly be represented by a landmark with a recognisable name association. But what landmark, and what name, if they were correct about Excalibur and the Lady of the Lake?

Suddenly they knew — a lake, a stretch of water. This must be it. Hurriedly they grabbed the map and spread it on the floor. A lake, but which of the several shown on the map?

Almost immediately they found it. A small lake just south of Worcester, about ten miles south-west of Huddington. Near enough almost certainly, and neither too near nor too far. Next to it stood a hill, *Knights Hill*. It must be! *Knights*. Knights of the Round Table, King Arthur, St. George, Knights slaying the dragon, the link, the final key connecting all the clues and symbolic indications. In some legends the Knights of the Round Table number nine. Other legends speak of the Nine Worthy Knights. (3)

But was the hill called Knights Hill in the seventeenth century? Next day they checked the maps at Worcester records library, but were unable to find any dating back to the time of Pakington. Nevertheless, it appeared that Knights Hill had been called that for many years, at least from Cromwellian times. They also discovered that the lake was known locally as Knights Pool. It stands secluded on the estate of Croome Court, once the home of the Earl of Coventry. If the Stone was there where was it hidden? On an island in the middle of the lake, buried in the earth banks, or in an old building overlooking it? The only construction was the remains of an old mill house, a relatively recent building.

That evening, Monday, 22 October, at around 8.30 p.m. the phone rang in the office. It was Alan Beard. To their astonishment he said they were not looking for a stone at this stage, but something that would ultimately lead them to it.

They were looking, he told them, for a sword, and added that once an old mill had stood near the place. Alan's psychic information was astounding. He knew nothing of the discoveries about Excalibur or the pool or, in fact, anything of the past days findings. And, even more amazingly, beside the pool there stood the remains of an old mill. Graham and Andy were flabbergasted by Alan's accuracy.

Andy told Alan what they had discovered, but said the journey to the pool could not be made until the following weekend.

Suddenly, Alan became uncharacteristically adamant. No, he said, they must go now. It couldn't wait. *Someone else was getting close, someone or something evil.* In the turmoil of the last few days they had forgotten the opposition that Joanna had warned them about.

Finally he gave them one last piece of information he was sure would help. Near where the sword was hidden there stood a solitary holly bush. Alan's message was too accurate to be coincidence. If he was right about the sword and the old mill, then he could be right about the opposition. Suddenly they remembered Marion's vision of a sword in water.

They could wait no longer.

Figure of King Arthur wielding excalibur. From the Nine Worthies at Harvington Hall.

Chapter Eight

The Silent Pool

QUICKLY they started gathering together warm clothes, torches, even swimming trunks and towels, in case they might have to dive into freezing waters should they find an island in the centre of the pool. Not really an engaging prospect, but they had to be prepared. The only digging equipment was their bare hands and a garden trowel. So they borrowed a spade from a neighbour.

As they travelled south towards Worcester, they began to wonder exactly what they might find once they reached Knights Pool. Not having had the chance to view the pool in daylight it would be doubly difficult to find their way by night. By deduction they guessed that the pool was only a few hundred yards outside the village of Severn Stoke.

Their first problem was how to avoid arrest for suspicious behaviour at the dead of night. Second, there was the pool itself. It was probably overgrown. The map indicated that it lay within a small wooded area. But how would they find their way in such restricting circumstances? Third, if the pool was on private land there would probably be no public right of way, or even access to it.

As they drew nearer to Severn Stoke, some forty miles away, they were in two minds whether to turn back and return to Wolverhampton. It was not yet 10.00 p.m. A pint of beer in cheerful surroundings would certainly be welcome.

They sat next to an old log fire in a wayside inn.

'D'you really think we need to go there tonight?' asked Graham.

Andy explained his feelings. He reasoned that if Joanna was right about the Stone and the pyschic messages were accurate, then there was no other alternative. So far everything had come true. Until that evening, neither had given much thought to the opposition of which all the psychics had spoken. Joanna had told them of a force of evil that the Stone could overcome, a power that had brought about the undoing of all those in history who had ever tried to oppose it.

'Look what happened to the Gunpowder Plotters,' said Graham. 'This power that was supposed to be on their side didn't do them much good, did it? We might find ourselves set up.'

'By who?' queried Andy.

'I don't know, but what about this opposition that Joanna spoke of? Others are also looking for the Stone, but from the other side.'

They had to admit it. The prospect of delving around in secluded woodland at midnight was rapidly losing its appeal.

The main reason they were on their way at all was the uncanny accuracy of Alan's message. He was right about what they knew, so the chances were that he was also right about someone else trying to find the Stone for themselves, or perhaps for this mysterious dark power.

Graham said: 'Where are we going to dig and how deep? We don't even know where to start?'

'Well,' said Andy, 'we've got a few choices. An island, if there is one, or Alan's mill house or holly bush, if it's still there.'

This was still not precise enough, for it left out too many other possibilities. In the back of their minds they wondered if they might not perhaps receive some psychic impression when the time was right. This led to another important issue.

If Alan and Marion had received psychic messages helping them to pinpoint the location of the Stone or possibly a sword, then from where had the messages originated? Joanna had claimed no knowledge of the whereabouts of the hidden artefact. And this was why they were searching for it in the first place, because it had apparently been lost. Where *did* the messages come from?

As the last orders were called it was almost as if they too were being called upon to make a decision. Should they go on? Of course. What else could they do? The decision was made. They would go ahead as planned and journey on to Knights Pool, prepared to face whatever lay ahead.

★   ★   ★   ★

Severn Stoke. The black lettering on the white-painted metal roadsign stood out in the car's headlamps. Neither of them spoke as they drove through the deserted main street. Only the occasional light from an upstairs window in the scattered cottages showed any evidence of life in the sleeping village. They passed through, not stopping for fear of attracting attention. In the darkness their thoughts returned once again to the opposition. Was someone else really searching for the Stone? Perhaps even at that very moment unseen eyes were following them.

They drove eastwards, following the rough dirt track that the map indicated led to the pool. After only a hundred yards it came to an abrupt end. The headlamp beams cast ghostly light on the trees ahead. This was it, the dark, unwelcoming woodland that surrounded Knights Pool.

Andy dowsed the lights as the engine cut out. They sat in the darkness, alone. Soon they left the vehicle, shining their torches round a small wooden stile next to it, leading to a narrow footpath through the dark trees into the wood.

They set off along the muddy patch, two dark silhouettes following the guiding light of a narrow torch beam. Suddenly there were no more trees, only darkness. The beams reflected off the black water as they found themselves on the banks of Knights Pool. They felt the cold rising from the empty expanse before them. The air was still, not even a light breeze through the trees nor the calling of some night creature broke the undisturbed solemnity of the quiet waters. It could hardly be called a pool, more like a small lake. Their torch beams swept like searchlights across the water, but still the glassy stillness revealed nothing. They could just make out the opposite bank, about thirty yards away. More marshy at the water's edge than on this side. Bulrushes and water grasses sprouted through the silt; the occasional dead tree with strangely contorted branches rose from the still waters with strands of dark vegetation hanging from them, like streamers on some long-forgotten Christmas tree.

They stood awhile on the banks, looking and listening. Everywhere silence, and blackness. By the light of their torches they could see that to the left the opposite bank came down to one end of the long, narrow pool. To their right the waters stretched away into the night.

'Well,' Graham whispered, 'what do you suggest?'

Andy leant forward as far as he could over the water, attempting to shine his torch further towards the far end of the lake obscured by the overhanging trees.

'We need to find out if there's an island in the pool, I suppose,' said Andy. 'Can't see anything up here.' They decided to follow the path further along. A small animal scurried away into the undergrowth as they moved forward, torches scanning quickly for any unnatural movement in the trees. After a short time the trees thinned, allowing a better view of the pool. Making their way to the water's edge once more they shone their torches across the lake. This time they could see the end of the lake.

'Now what?' said Graham. 'There's no island, so that possibility's eliminated.'

'Let's try to find the old mill, if we can,' said Andy. 'And, if possible, a holly bush.'

'But there might be hundreds of them,' Graham protested, 'although I haven't seen one yet.'

'Maybe there isn't one at all.' said Andy, and he pointed his torch towards the end of the lake. The beam illuminated some brickwork. It was a small bridge, half overgrown with thick brambles and semi-obscured by bushes. Here the pathway crossed over to the opposite side of the lake, and they followed it onto the slightly humped bridge under which water slowly trickled. As far as they could make out, it came from a small stream which fed the lake.

Standing on the bridge they peered towards the far end of the pool. It appeared to be about a hundred yards away. All around was quiet and still. They were alone in the darkness.

'D'you really think someone else could be making their way here?' asked Graham.

'If they are they'll see us a mile off with these bloody torches,' said Andy.

What would happen if someone did come? Neither could explain their increasing sense of urgency. Imagination? Yet there persisted the disturbing and unshakeable feeling that someone was coming nearer.

'Where's the mill?'

'Presumably it's a water mill.'

'Then there must be a stream leading out of the pool. Quiet.'

They listened carefully. A soft breeze had now risen and brushed gently through the trees. A bird splashed suddenly on the waters, and a moving car could be heard in the distance. But no hint of running water.

They continued round the lake, following the path along the other bank. As they walked the trees thinned until they could hear the sound of trickling water. The sound grew louder and more distinct. They moved toward it, Andy leading the way as Graham swept the opposite bank with his torch, checking if anyone else was approaching from where they had just come.

The torch picked out an area of stone rubble. Old grey stones scattered round a little stream that filtered from the pool.

'My God,' Andy said, 'this must be it.' In pieces on the floor were parts of the old grind stone, while all that remained of the mill were several piles of moss-covered brickwork. He picked up some bricks and shook his head.

'What's wrong?' asked Graham.

'I don't think this mill is going to help us. Look at these, they're much too new. A hundred years old at the most. And even if I'm wrong, if there ever was anything hidden here it's certainly gone now. Hardly anything left of it.' Andy shook his head. 'Either way I think we can count out the mill.'

'What about the holly bush?' said Graham. 'It seems our last hope.' He started to leave, but Andy didn't follow. Graham turned and shone his torch at Andy. He stood quite still, staring out across the lake.

'What the hell is it?' asked Graham.

For a moment Andy didn't answer. 'Pakington logic,' he said. 'We're forgetting to think Pakington logic. We've become too damn pre-occupied with Alan's message. He gave us enough to guide us to the right track, but he never said where the sword was hidden.'

'Go on,' Graham prompted, returning to the site of the mill.

'Where would Pakington have hidden the sword? There's no island in the pool, so where else?'

'How can we guess that in the dark,' protested Graham. 'If there's another old building somewhere round here it could be some distance away.'

'If Pakington used it, it would be nearby, I'd guess,' said Andy.

They searched again. The minutes passed and turned to hours

while they grew colder and colder. They were tempted to leave and return in the daylight, but somehow they knew that if they did they would return to find nothing. The urgency in Alan's voice troubled them still. *They knew they had to find it tonight.*

A sword, Alan had said. They were looking for a sword. In their imagination the night played strange tricks. Everywhere they saw swords, erect branches, mysterious shadows. Then, just as they were about to give up and leave they saw it.

'The holly tree,' cried Andy. A large single holly tree stood beside the path, twenty or so yards from the bridge. Was this what Alan had seen? Could this really be where the sword was buried? It was a large holly tree, not a bush, but good enough.

They began digging.

'D'you think it could be the bridge,' Andy said slowly. 'It's the only structure around the pool. If it was there in Pakington's day then it overlooked the pool. What better place.'

It was possible. The holly tree was nearby. They transferred their attentions to the bridge. Here the slowly moving stream passed beneath. Long grass and soil covered the bridge, thick turf above the red brick arch rising about four feet over the waters below. Bulrushes grew alongside it. The foundations were matted with successive layers of branches and undergrowth.

Graham leant cautiously over the edge and shone his torch beneath the arch.

'No way,' his voice echoed from below.

'What is it?' said Andy. Graham pulled himself up. 'I can't see this bridge dating back to Pakington. It's just not old enough. The red brickwork is too modern.' He cleared his throat. 'It can't possibly be three hundred and fifty years old. Besides, bridges have to be repaired, so they're hardly likely to be much of a hiding place.'

Andy leant over the edge and pointed his torch into the undergrowth on either side.

'Hold on a moment,' he cried.

'What is it?'

'Some of these foundation stones look pretty ancient.'

They clambered down the side of the bridge and under the arch, crouching painfully on a narrow ledge only inches above the freezing waters. They examined the brickwork. Certainly the foundations appeared to be much older. Large, irregularly hewn stonework. As far as they could see the foundations to both sides of the arch were of the same roughly-hewn stones. How old these foundations were they had no way of telling, but there was little doubt they were of much older construction, completely different from the red house-bricks of the arch itself. The arch had obviously been repaired. They scrabbled out and back onto the bridge again.

'D'you think it's possible that this bridge does date back to Pakington's time?' Graham asked.

'Apart from the arch it's certainly very old,' Andy replied. They moved back and forth, examining the bridge still further. Andy's 'Pakington logic' echoed in their ears. If something had been hidden by Humphrey Pakington, Gertrude Wyntour, or whoever, and if Knights Pool was the place alluded to by the Nine Worthies, then where would the artefact be hidden? Had there been an island then surely he would have chosen that. But no island was to be seen. So where else? If the bridge had stood in his time it would be the obvious choice.

Suddenly it struck them. Even though bridges need repairing, their foundations remain. Here the foundations to either side were completely covered by years of vegetation.

The prickly brambles and creepers scratched viciously as they hacked a path through to the stones. One side of the bridge seemed well preserved, whilst the opposite side was quite dilapidated. It was the side facing the lake that was in the best state of preservation. No doubt following heavy rainfall, the flooding waters would gush under the bridge and, over the years, cause more damage to this side. The lakeward side would not have suffered such batterings, and presumably Pakington would have reasoned this out, taking the precaution to bury nothing on the riverward side. Perhaps somewhere on the side nearest the lake there lay buried the artefact they sought.

'I suppose it would make sense for him to hide something in the side of the bridge overlooking the pool,' said Graham, 'assuming he chose the bridge. But which side and where?'

'Behind a stone, maybe,' said Andy. 'They're certainly big enough to hide something behind.'

'Yes, but which one?'

Andy thought for a moment. 'So many down and so many across perhaps?' he suggested.

'But how many?'

Andy thought again. 'Got it!' he said. 'The number of the Worthies, of course. Nine.' It seemed too easy. Yet why not; logically that would be what the Nine Worthies would have represented. Pakington logic once again.

They stood on the bridge, deliberating their best course of action. They agreed there was a good possibility that if there was a buried sword, then the bridge must be the hiding place. But they were badly equipped to begin removing stones from the foundations. They were too solidly fixed, and they would need help. More importantly they needed to find out about the bridge. For a start, whose land was it on? Whose permission must they seek?

They were caught between what they should or should not do. Alan had been too accurate for it to be a coincidence, and he had been right about what they had found so far. In addition, he had stressed the urgency. Over and over they discussed the situation, and everything that had happened to date which had led them to the bridge on this cold, dark autumn night.

If they hesitated would it be too late? Alan Beard certainly thought so. Everything else had been right. The psychic messages, uncannily accurate. The historical information, totally correct. They could not afford to leave, they owed it to the psychics, to all those involved.

The bridge was indeed in a state of ill repair, clearly undisturbed for many years. Completely overgrown, and on the river side crumbling away into decay. Another stone or two carefully removed and replaced could surely do no harm. They had to try it.

'From where should we count the stones, along, up or across?' asked Graham, again leaning out over the edge. Andy joined him, shining his torch at the foundations. He began counting.

'Nine from the bridge from where the centre arch gives way to the side supports, I'd think.'

Graham agreed.

'And nine down would put it deep in the foundation, safer than just a few stones from the top.'

They now had to decide which side. It was a toss up, but perhaps the swords of the Nine Worthies, since they were pointing to the right when viewed straight on, indicated the right-hand side of the bridge as it faced the lake. They chose that side. Here it was even

more overgrown than the rest of the bridge, with almost impenetrable brambles, high nettles, thick weed and creepers. They took
turns holding the torch as the other hacked away at the
undergrowth with a stick. Eventually they were forced to return to
the car to collect the spade.

After some time they reached the edge of the wall which comprised the side foundations of the bridge. The side was equally
overgrown, both from the top and bottom.

Their hands were painful with cuts and nettle stings, but their
work was far from being completed. Next they had to clear the
thick, twisting vegetation from the stone work itself, exposing the
bridge for perhaps the first time in years. They jumped onto a band
of soft ground below, dividing the bridge from the black mud and
water of the lake. They cleared away the remaining creepers which
still clung to the lichen covered stone work. The old wall was
exposed before them, each stone about a foot wide and six or so
inches high. It was then that they recalled the smell of rotting
vegetation that Marion had told them about when she had her
vision of the sword. Where they crouched the stench of decay was
almost overpowering.

Quickly they counted the stones and found the one they wanted.
Like the other stones it was fixed firmly in place.

'Shall we try to move it?' Andy asked.

Graham glanced around. The cold, dark lake lay silent behind
them. Again they felt a mounting sense of urgency, a kind of fear.
Were they on the brink of discovering something that would once
and for all convince them of the reality of the strange psychic
messages, perhaps even change their lives? Or would there just be
nothing?

Graham held the torch as Andy scraped away at the moss-filled
crevice around the stone. The age old cement behind it was more
difficult to remove than they had expected. For nearly half an hour
they took turns in digging away at it, alternately using Andy's
penknife and trowel. They had to also loosen several of the
surrounding stones. After some little time the stone moved a
fraction, and they were able to get a grip, rocking it to and fro,
heaving and pushing to loosen it further, scraping their mud-
covered fingers in the process. The growing anticipation
overshadowed their pain and discomfort. Then, with a final tug the

stone came away, bringing with it a shower of debris.

Andy shone his torch into the black hole. There was something there! Something was lying on the narrow recess behind the stone which had fallen away, still partly hidden by an adjoining stone. Although encrusted with years of silt and earth deposits its shape could still be made out, *the shape of a long dagger or short sword*.

Alan had been right! A sword. No! It was impossible. They had followed the trail of clues and psychic messages, but neither of them had ever really believed it could happen. How could they? No, it couldn't be a sword, it was impossible. The dim light of the torches in the recess was playing tricks. They had been thinking about swords for too long.

They continued to stare, but the earth-covered shape did not fade to become a protruding root or crack in the rock. It was still as they had first seen it. It was real. No fantasy. They stared in disbelief. It was true.

What Joanna had said, Marion's psychic visions, the psychic messages, all must be true. There was no other explanation. Graham felt his stomach muscles tighten. He had never denied the existence of psychic phenomena. But this ... It was not simply the realisation of the truth of the psychic messages, but all that it implied. Here was the final proof.

Nor could Andy control his emotions. He lost control and burst into tears. Tears of relief, shock, or joy he didn't know which. He turned and shook Graham by the shoulders. Graham turned and stared blankly, his eyes wide and unseeing.

'It's here,' Andy cried. 'It's bloody here! I don't believe it.'

Yet neither of them attempted to touch the object.

'I thought I was dreaming,' said Graham.

'So did I. You can see it. I've been seeing swords everywhere.',

'Me, too.'

They stared at each other. Andy wiped a mud-covered arm across his face. They exchanged an unspoken question. Who would be first to pick it up?

Graham stretched out his hand and touched it. It was real, he could feel its rough texture. He brought it into full view and withdrew it, holding it at arm's length, somehow not wanting to hold it too close.

It was about twenty inches long, the tapering blade about two-thirds of that length. A small cross-piece, perhaps of two inches, divided the hilt from the blade. No details could be made out through the encrusted silt. A long dagger or short sword, either way Alan had been right. Graham handed it to Andy, almost reverently.

It *was* true. But *what* was true? What force, what power, what intelligence lay behind it? UFO beings, a living woman speaking through a medium, an ancient secret sect? How did it all fit? And why should they be the ones to find the sword? And what about the Stone? That must also surely exist. But where? The Stone that held the power to overcome some force of evil, a force of evil that . . . . The realisation that this force must also exist hit them between the eyes. It had already destroyed so many. It too, wanted to possess the Stone. Maybe it wanted to destroy it, or was its intention even more sinister? It wanted the Stone, perhaps, for its own evil ends.

Joanna had said there were others, mortals like themselves, who had been inspired by that opposing force to search for the Stone. Alan had stressed the urgency. He had said someone else was getting close. But this opposition, who were they, where were they?

Their eyes searched the dark lake, the black silhouettes of the trees against the moonlit night sky. They were alone, and vulnerable.

'For God's sake, Andy, let's get out of here,' urged Graham, in a desperate whisper.

Andy glanced round 'D'you think. . . .' Graham did not let him finish.

'I don't know what I think. All I know is that anyone, anything, God knows what, could be on its way here.'

They quickly checked the recess for anything else, replaced the stones and hurried back to the car, all the while looking behind them as they left the scene of the most shattering experience of their lives.

Chapter Nine

———————◆———————

Meonia fore Marye

THEY found themselves bolting the door and checking the windows in the headquarters. Every small sound jarred their senses, sounds they would normally have ignored or perhaps not even heard.

They laid the encrusted sword on a sheet of paper spread out on the table. It looked singularly unimpressive, a long metal object covered in dried earth.

It was three o'clock in the morning. What should they do? Contact Terry perhaps. But somehow they felt it might be unwise to speak over the phone. A plethora of ideas flashed through their minds, some crazy, some not so crazy. Were they being watched, or bugged? Quickly they rationalized the situation; back in familiar surroundings they could see things in better perspective.

Alan had said that the sword would ultimately lead them to the Stone. The only way to find out was to remove the sediment from the sword. But if they tried to clean it would they damage it? Should they take it to local archaeologists or historians, experts who could advise them on the correct procedure to avoid damaging their precious find? If the sword was to lead to the Meonia Stone, with time running out, there was no choice but to clean it immediately.

A pocket knife removed the deposits fairly easily, as a small lump fell away to reveal the dull-grey metal surface. It looked to be remarkably well preserved, with no signs of corrosion. It was covered by what appeared to be some form of resin, and it was this that had enabled them to easily remove the sediment. Whoever had hidden the sword had certainly ensured its preservation. They had

73

probably immersed it in some kind of wax or lacquer. In places this protective sheath had remained impermanent, and patches of minor corrosion could be seen. Piece by piece the sediment came away, gradually revealing the naked sword. It appeared to be cast metal, the hilt, cross-piece and blade forged together from what looked to be steel. It was certainly not gold or silver. They had half expected to find it encrusted with jewels. Instead, it was a single-cast steel dagger, the hilt decorated with rings and indentations. Simple decorative markings adorned the cross guard, and where this joined the hilt they could see two separate devices or crests on either side. One side could not be clearly distinguished, but the other appeared to show Roman numerals and an unidentifiable marking.

'There's something here,' said Andy, excitedly, scraping away the upper section of the blade to reveal the grey surface. He tilted the sword into the light. 'Look, there's something written on the blade.' He hurriedly picked off the remaining sediment as Graham fetched a table lamp. They examined the lettering closely, and saw three separate words inscribed along the blade some two centimetres from the hilt.

Andy spelt out the first of the words. 'M ... E ... something ..I ...A . Good grief! *Meonia. Meonia for Mary,*' he exclaimed.

Meonia. The word Joanna had used for the Stone; The Meonia Stone. There could be no doubt that the words read *MEONIA FORE MARYE.*

Graham shook his head slowly. 'I'd half convinced myself it was a ridiculous coincidence,' he said. 'The sword being there. I mean it could have been an old builder's trademark, or perhaps a good-luck custom. But the word Meonia on the blade, that clinches it.'

They cleaned the rest of the blade and placed the sword on the table. There were no more markings or messages, so how did this short metal sword hold the key to the Meonia Stone? Was there perhaps something hidden inside the sword itself? It was solid cast so it seemed unlikely. If the sword held the clue to the discovery of the Stone then the key would very probably be the words *Meonia fore Marye*. But now it was too late to do anything more. Too tired to think they retired to snatch a few hours sleep. Andy slept on the couch in the front room with the sword safely hidden beneath it.

Graham could not sleep. For over an hour he stared from the bedroom window into the darkness of the early morning. After a time he forced himself to sleep, but after only half an hour he awoke, unable to relax as a thousand questions rushed through his mind.

★   ★   ★

He ran. His clothes were strange. She had never seen him before. He ran swiftly, glancing back to check he was not being followed. He must not be waylaid, nothing must hinder his task. She was close behind, following as he travelled, dragging his feet heavily through the marshy landscape. Then, leaving the boggy ground, he moved swiftly across fields, through waterlogged pastures and tall grass meadows. The rain cascaded from the dark clouds, billowing in sheets against the passing trees and hedgerows, driving down on the runner. Yet still he ran, over high fences and across flooded ditches filled with gushing muddy waters. She knew he could not stop. But how, how could she know? What had brought her to this troubled place?

He paused at a low stile, glancing anxiously along the mud-swamped trackway. He must stay clear of the roads. It was too risky, too dangerous. He might be seen, or caught. He must keep to the fields and unfrequented tracks, travelling cross-country as long as possible.

He jumped from the stile and set off once more, following the narrow lane down a long avenue of trees from which the pounding rain sprayed viciously. He was cold and tired, his clothes stained and torn. But he must not rest, not even for a moment. It was not far now, not far.

She knew that she must follow the lonely figure. There was something she must do, something she had to know.

Again he left the track, through a broken wooden gate and across the meadows, saturated and heavy with the smell of decay. His tired feet sank deep into the mud and he stumbled frequently, each step an almost insurmountable barrier of pain. He drove on, force of will taking him onto the high ground where it was firm. Continuing across the rain-spattered fields, through sheltered woodlands and again risking the dangerous trackways, he at last reached his destination.

Breathing heavily he turned. Still he did not see her as she watched him, gasping for breath on the narrow stone bridge. This was the place. Only now did she catch sight of it, something hidden from view inside a bundle of cloth clasped tightly to his chest. Then he was gone. For a time she was alone. His head and shoulders suddenly appeared over the side of the bridge as he fumbled and dragged himself back onto the pathway. He no longer held the cloth. She knew that he had hidden whatever it was that had lain inside.

Gaynor sat up in bed, She felt her arms. They were dry, but how? It was raining. Raining? How could it be raining? She was inside her bedroom at home! It had just been a dream. But something told her that it was no ordinary dream. She must tell someone. But why, what could it mean?

It was still dark outside. Her little sister was fast asleep in her bed, breathing softly and deeply. Gaynor lay back, listening to the familiar sound. She felt sleepy. Not to worry, she would tell her mother in the morning.

★ ★ ★ ★

Graham and Andy had eventually managed to snatch a few hours of sleep. After a hasty lunch they were again on the move, this time delivering copies of the *Parasearch* magazine to local wholesalers.

In the early evening they phoned Terry and Marion to say they would be over on the following day. But Marion was impatient to hear of the latest developments.

When they arrived at Terry's they were joined by Alan. The two men sat in silence as Graham and Andy recounted the events of the previous evening. Alan stared in disbelief at the sword.

'What about the sword? D'you know what it's for?' asked Graham.

Alan shook his head.

Over dinner the main topic of conversation was the cryptic message *Meonia fore Marye*. What did it mean and how could it lead to the Stone? Who was *Marye*? Mary Queen of Scots perhaps? And what was the meaning of the word *Meonia*?

They spoke openly in front of Terry's wife Pat, but were careful not to mention anything about an opposition or supernatural conflict. For the time being the discovery was purely the result of psychic archaeology. Terry's concern for Pat's disbelief was unfounded; in the coming months she too was to become involved in the ever more bizarre events.

'We've got to be very careful,' suggested Terry, his parting words to Graham and Andy as they left. 'Careful who we talk to. For the time being, anyway, until we know more about this opposition.'

'If they exist,' Andy emphasised, leaning from the car window.

'The sword exists,' Alan said, as they drove away and headed towards Marion's.

They arrived around mid-evening, to be greeted with news of a still stranger twist to the affair. Before they had a chance to explain anything to Marion, she told them the details of Gaynor's dream. She described the man, in old-fashioned clothes, running across country and hiding some unseen object in the foundations of an old bridge.

Andy and Graham were astonished. Marion knew nothing of their find, and Gaynor herself had not even been told that they were searching for something. So Alan Beard was not the only one to receive psychic information about the location of the sword. Gaynor, too, had somehow witnessed the actual moment of hiding it, perhaps by Humphrey Pakington in 1605.

The implications of Alan and Gaynor receiving such accurate psychic impressions were disturbing. It suggested that *something* appeared to have known the precise location of the sword and divulged psychic information to both of them. But if something really knew, why had they not been told? Where did the psychic visions, messages and impressions originate?

They told Marion the whole story. Once again she seemed to have been expecting it.

'Any idea what it might mean?' Andy asked her, as she examined the inscription. She was about to answer, but her expression suddenly changed and she looked up.

'There's something here,' she said, glancing about her. 'Can't you feel it?'

They shook their heads.

'What is it?' asked Graham.

'I don't know,' she answered, then fell silent again. Andy and Graham watched as she reclined in her armchair. There was silence as the two men exchanged glances.

'Marion?' said Andy, 'are you all right?' There was no reply. They waited. It seemed that Marion had fallen into a trance state similar to those that had resulted in the Joanna communications. Her face changed as an uncharacteristic frown tightened across her brow. The muscles at each side of her mouth began to twitch. She spoke, her voice unchanged except that her accent was gone.

Her eyes opened wide and stared at them. For some minutes she spoke without faltering, addressing them directly and by name but allowing no time for any replies.

There was much they and others would be called upon to do, she

77

said. Those who were to find and possess the Stone were to prepare for a task to oppose a force beyond their capabilities to understand fully.

'Who are you?' Graham urged. The voice did not reply. 'Do you know where the Stone is?' Still she did not reply. 'Can you tell us why we have been called upon to do this?'

'I can only tell you this,' she said slowly. 'The seeds of destruction lie within.'

The trance was over. Afterwards she seemed partly to remember what had occurred, but was at a total loss to explain it. She was worried at having fallen into an involuntary trance, although she felt no ill effects.

What had spoken through Marion Sunderland? Was this yet another guise of the chameleon intelligence that lay behind the whole affair? And what was meant by 'the seeds of destruction lie within?' It seemed like a warning.

A little later Marion agreed to attempt to 'tune in' to the source of the psychic messages in an effort to obtain more information about the whereabouts of the Meonia Stone.

'Nothing,' she said. 'I'm sorry, but it doesn't seem to work as simply as that.' She closed her eyes again, attempting to clear her mind. 'Yes, there is something,' She began. 'I can see something now. It's a horse, a white horse ... and something else I can't make out.' She shielded her eyes with the palms of her hands. 'Yes,' she half shouted. 'It's a row of trees, an avenue, over there,' she indicated with her hand, 'stretching away. There's an old track between them, and water, it's near water.' She suddenly gasped. 'It's here, I'm sure of it. The Stone, it's here!'

About now some important historical facts about the Gunpowder Plot and the Rosicrucian era were discovered, which enabled them to theorize as to why the Rosicrucians had wanted to become involved with the English Catholics. And more importantly how Robert Catesby might have come to possess the Meonia Stone that meant so much to a protestant Order in Germany.

From what they could discover it seemed that the Rosicrucians of 1605 considered Princess Elizabeth, the nine-year-old daughter of

James I, to be a long-prophecied leader, the future Queen who was to lead a newly-enlightened Europe. Elizabeth, however, was not the immediate heir to the English throne. (1)

For many years mystical and occult texts had circulated throughout Europe announcing that the New Age was at hand, an age of intellectual freedom. These manuscripts were often accompanied by illustrations depicting the New Age as a young woman or girl riding on horseback to oppose tyranny. (2) The Rosicrucians, it seems, considered Elizabeth to be the personification of this symbol. Some years after the Gunpowder Plot, in 1613, when Elizabeth married Frederick V. of the Palatinate, the Rosicrucian manifestos proclaimed this as the grand alliance. The New Age was at hand. But the dream collapsed with Elizabeth and Frederick's rash attempt to secure the throne of Bohemia and so oppose the Hapsburgs, one of the greatest of the sovereign dynasties of Europe. (3)

In 1605, however, Elizabeth was still the 'chosen one', the embodiment of hope for the reformist Rosicrucians, since during the previous year two new stars had appeared in the constellations of Cygnus, the Swan, and Serpentarius, the Snake. This was taken by the Rosicrucians to be additional proof that the New Age was at hand. (4)

It had been Princess Elizabeth whom the Gunpowder Plotters had wanted to place on the English throne. She had been the cornerstone of the entire plot. Was it possible that the Rosicrucians had come to an agreement with Catesby and the other English Catholics? A plan to enthrone Elizabeth with the promise of religious freedom and toleration, necessitating Catesby having the Stone to assure his success? Had Catesby, overwhelmed at possessing the Meonia Stone, devised his own mad scheme, the true extent of which was unknown to the Rosicrucians until too late? After all, most of the Catholics who offered their support to Catesby failed to realise what he was planning. A rebellion, yes, but to murder the King and his entire Parliament. Never!

For the first time since the strange events had started Alan was afraid. He felt he recognised the opposition, or at least what was involved: *Witchcraft*. Graham, Terry and Andy could not believe it, but the more they considered it the more likely it seemed. If the force that the Stone could overcome was evil, it followed that such a force would use those practising the black arts.

Graham and Andy had investigated many stories about the beliefs of modern witches, but until now they had not given serious thought to the claims of the witch cult. With the growing confusion of the past few weeks they were no longer quite so ready to scoff. Could their opposition include a group practising witchcraft? Any thought concerning this possibility might have rested there, had Andy not paid a visit to a London bookseller.

On Friday morning he called in to see a bookshop specialising in the paranormal, where he ran across a magazine feature about a witchcraft murder that had taken place on St. Valentine's day 1945.

He already knew some of the details of this unsolved crime: a man found dead in a field in the Warwickshire countryside. The victim, Charles Walton, a resident of the village of Lower Quinton, was discovered pinned to the ground by his own hay fork, with the sign of a cross slashed across his throat. The style of this savage murder caused the police to consider whether Walton had not been ritualistically murdered by a sect of witches. Scotland Yard detectives called on the country's leading occult authorities to help identify the murderers. However, after many months investigations the case remained unsolved.

When Andy was reminded of the name of the hill on which Walton had been found he bought the magazine and hurriedly left the shop.

Walton's body had been discovered on *Meon* Hill. Meon — Meonia. Coincidence perhaps? He could afford to ignore nothing when so much was at stake.

For two weeks everyone had tried to discover the meaning of the word Meonia. Why was it called the *Meonia* Stone? Since the mysterious engraving read *Meonia fore Marye*, they all felt that Meonia held the key for which they were looking. But nowhere was such a word to be found.

Now Andy had been reminded of Meon Hill. What did Meon mean? More interesting still was the proximity of Meon Hill to Huddington, the home of Gertrude Wyntour, a mere fifteen miles away.

Meon Hill had been so named long before the Gunpowder Plot,

and therefore it was likely that Pakington and Gertrude would have known of it. So here was a recognisable name-association on a permanent landmark: Pakington logic. But was the Stone hidden on Meon Hill? The idea was tempting.

The magazine feature stated that there had been much speculation about Walton having been a member of the witch coven which had murdered him, and that he had been killed because he had refused to return something he had been entrusted with. And the object was a gem, a mystical stone.

They all now harboured the same inescapable thought. Had somebody already located the Meonia Stone, possibly a coven of witches around Meon Hill many years ago? Had this group already found the stone, while all they had was Pakington's indicator, probably hidden as an afterthought? But if it had been found, why did Joanna not know? They were certain on one point. If a coven of witches had located the Meonia Stone in the 1940s, it was unlikely to be the coven now working for their unnamed adversary. Joanna would have known this.

Alan's message about a witch coven had by now received further support from Marion, who had herself received powerful visual images of strange ceremonies and satanic rites. But she had seen even more. She felt she had been given a glimpse of their chief rival, a woman in her forties, with long black hair. John Avis and John Ward also said that they had had psychic impressions of a woman of similar appearance who was and the High Priestess of a strange and fanatical sect. These new and disturbing messages, plus Andy's findings about the Meon Hill killing, made them want to give it all up. Forget the quest, and the messages and leave well alone. But how could they? Fate had already taken them too far. How long would it be before their adversaries glimpsed psychic impressions of *them*?

For the first time they took Joanna's plea for urgent action very seriously. They had until 31 October to find the Stone. It was now the twenty-sixth. Time was desperately short.

Andy introduced Alan and Terry to Marion and Fred at their home on the evening of Friday 26 October. Joined by Graham and a friend, Janet Morgan, they talked into the early hours.

Where was the Meonia Stone? Time and time again they examined the sword. What did the inscription mean, what was it indicating? The possibilites were many, but clearly Meon Hill was their best lead. They also discovered that the area surrounding Meon Hill and Lower Quinton had an ancient tradition of witchcraft. There were rumours of a coven near Meon Hill which occasionally met for ceremonies at a prehistoric stone circle called the Rollright Stones.

Joanna had said they must find the Stone by 31 October, Hallow-een, the major witch festival of the year. Either they or their adversaries must succeed by that date. Marion was most concerned.

'We're on the right track,' she said 'but we've got it wrong.'

'In what way?' Alan asked.

'I don't think the Stone has been found. I definitely saw where it was. I'm sure of that. By the avenue of trees I described. I'm certain it's still hidden.'

'So what about Charles Walton and whatever it was that he was supposed to have had?' asked Andy. 'Has that nothing to do with it?'

'I think the Meon Hill murder has something to do with what we're up against. I don't know how I know, but I'm sure something is trying to get a message to us.'

She explained how she felt that the dark-haired woman she had seen was the head of the coven that met at the Rollrights stone circle, but they were not a third party. Rather they were the group who also sought the Meonia Stone. Perhaps, she suggested, they had stayed for years near Meon Hill because they believed that this was where the Stone was hidden. She was sure that the evil force — the evil being that Joanna had spoken of — had for years been manipulating this coven, hoping that they would one day discover the Meonia Stone. Why they hadn't found the sword she didn't know. She also felt that there was more to the sword than they yet understood, that its secret was still to be revealed.

Besides, *Joanna* had told them of the Nine Worthies and of Pakington's involvement. Perhaps Joanna's evil opposition only knew of Gertrude Wyntour's involvement, and so never knew of the coded message at Harvington Hall.

'I think there is another stone,' said Marion. 'What Walton had was something different, *their* stone if you like.'

Alan nodded in agreement. 'D'you think their stone could do us any harm?' he asked.

Marion nodded, 'I think it could.'

'This might sound rather weird,' Alan said, 'but the words "beware of the round stone" came into my mind the other day. I don't know if it's relevant.'

No-one seemed to know. Marion said that she had had a further impression, that the coven headed by this dark-haired woman would meet at the Rollright Stones on Halloween for some evil purpose. She *knew* that they must find the Stone by the night of Halloween, and use it to put an end to her powers. But her coven was also looking for the Stone, and they now had the means of finding it. Marion felt that the coven had in some way been alerted by Joanna's communication. Perhaps it was for this reason that Joanna had not been able to tell them where the sword was hidden; instead she could only alert them to the clues to set them on the right path. But if Joanna knew and was a living woman, why had she not collected the sword herself? They did not know.

Marion felt that some of the psychic messages had been intercepted, but that their adversaries were unaware that they had already found the sword. Before they broke up Alan and Marion had a simultaneous impression that something was searching for them. They could feel it, getting nearer and nearer. Soon it would find them.

There were five days left in which to find the Meonia Stone.

Meon Hill stood out ominously against the horizon as they approached that Sunday morning. The gradual incline contrasted sharply with the cloudless sky beyond. Only the small cluster of trees that marked the summit broke the even skyline. These lonely copses, standing high above the rolling terrain were, legend has it, first planted centuries ago by the Druids, thus creating temples of nature for their secret rites. Wooded groves where the ancients called upon the forces of nature. Folklore and country tales hold the last vestiges of these age-old mysteries. Tales of the heroic deeds of Celtic warriors who once stood watch on the ramparts of the Iron Age hill-fort that now lies overgrown and forgotten on the upland beside the wood. A silent guardian of the easternmost gateway to the fertile Vale of Evesham, Meon Hill looks out over the tiny market gardens and peaceful orchards dotted across the countryside as it sweeps away into the west.

Satan himself, so legend tells, had created Meon Hill. In a moment of rage he cast a huge clod of earth in the hope of destroying the great Abbey of Evesham. But God had intervened and the Devil threw too far; the pile of earth had crashed some nine miles to the east, and so created what is now the mount of Meon Hill.

The village of Lower Quinton appeared anything but sinister as they parked their car for a clearer view of the hill before them. Andy, Graham and Janet discussed their next move, finding it difficult to believe that somewhere in the area there might exist a satanic order of witches, a diabolical cult who had killed once and could, if the need arose, kill again.

They decided to drive on, following the maze of narrow country lanes running part of the way up the hillside. They scanned the surrounding landscape, searching for Marion's avenue of trees — their only clue. They followed the road until it ended and parked on the grass verge beside an old farm gate. Clambering over the fence and following the narrow pathway alongside the recently harvested field they climbed the gentle slopes toward the summit of the hill. From here they had a panoramic view of the countryside, but nowhere was there an avenue of trees. Perhaps the local church held some clue. The architectural style told them it was old, built well before the days of the Gunpowder Plot. Maybe it was dedicated to St. Mary. *Meonia fore Marye*, was that the meaning of the message? But unless the church could offer further clues there was little point in starting to dig indiscriminately.

Graham and Janet studied the map as Andy went off in search of the hill-fort remains. They discussed the reality of the witch coven. There was no actual proof. Then again, nearly all the psychics had experienced visions and messages about the coven.

Finally they arrived at a decision. If the messages were accurate then it was better to know their enemy. But where to begin? If, as Marion claimed, the coven were to meet at the Rollright Stones in less than three days time, they would now be making preparations for their satanic rites.

They decided to go to the Rollright Stones but, before leaving, they checked in the church. There was nothing of interest.

What, they wondered, lay ahead of them as they drove away from Meon Hill towards the ancient stone circle? The tranquility of the sunny afternoon did little to dispel their mounting fears.

Chapter Ten

———————◆———————

Race Against Time

*T*HE *incense smoke spiralled upwards from the altar. Defiant points of yellow light from the candles adorned the image of Our Lady. The old priest solemnly led his tiny congregation in prayer. The feeling of safety and reassurance, the serenity of the church.*

But something else broke in upon that holy sanctuary. A sense of something vile, something wicked and immeasurably evil. Gaynor felt a dark shadow falling around her. She shuddered, trying to fight it off. She looked at her two younger brothers who were still singing. Her little sister stared innocently up at her. She knew they could not feel it; knew she was alone. Why would it not leave? What did it want with her?

She tried to concentrate on the priest's voice, to fight it off. That kindly voice, no evil could defy his loving concern. A greater power operated through him, guiding and inspiring his words. But the shadow fell between them, blanketing his words with a heavy curtain of darkness. How could something so wicked enter the house of God?

Then she knew. No evil approached her. She felt the now familiar love of her 'friends'. They were calling her. There was something evil, but not in the chapel, not about her. Her 'friends' wished her to see it, she was being alerted, warned. The evil she had felt jarring at her nerves was far away in some distant place. They wished her to see it. They were sad, sorry that she must be shown, but only she could help. Gaynor agreed. She was willing to see.

The darkness melted away to reveal a scene, somewhere terribly old. Once, good things had taken place there; there had been joy, the lore of nature, happy people. But this was no more. There had been atrocities against nature, acts of cruelty. Now evil lurked there, a dark shadow covered everything. What was this place? Gnarled and contorted shapes. Grey figures in a ring, silently waiting. As the light by which she saw grew in brightness Gaynor could see that the shapes were not people but cold stone, a circle of standing stones. How could they do this? Who had filled this place with such evil, and transformed it into a desecrated sanctuary?

Then she saw the woman, her long, black hair flowing wildly in the wind. She was not young although she was still beautiful. But her eyes, the windows to her soul, betrayed her. Bottomless pits of darkness they shone no beauty, only blackness. She was the instrument of some terrifying force which through her worked unimaginable cruelty.

In her hands she held something, something she was making. An intertwined ring, a crown of thorns, a sacriligious offering between which she wove sprigs of black and red berries, beads of deadly poison. A mockery of all that was good. Gaynor almost felt the bitter contempt of the woman as she placed this blasphemous token on the stone slab with a parody of loving care.

Why should she be shown such wickedness? Again she was answered. The scene faded and she saw familiar faces, people she knew. Graham, Andy and Janet. They were smiling, but she knew they were heading for danger, great danger. They were drawing nearer, closer to this evil, a power they did not understand, which could destroy them.

Gaynor almost cried their names aloud. She must tell them, stop them. But how?

★ ★ ★ ★

Seven long strides shall thou take
If Long Compton thou canst see
King of England thou shalt be . . .

are the words a conquering King was said to have heard as he approached the crest of the hill outside Long Compton on his triumphant march through England. The witch who owned the hill had set him this task, but as the King marched forward a mound of earth rose up blocking his view of the village. He and his knights were turned to stone with the words:

As Long Compton thou can'st not see
King of England thou shalt not be
Rise up stick, and stand still, stone,
For King of England thou shalt be none.
Thou and thy men hoar stones shall be
And I myself an eldern tree . . .

The Rollright Stones legend has existed for more than four centuries, and over the years the old stone circle has become the traditional meeting place of the witches for which Long Compton was notorious. Embedded deep in the earth of the hill overlooking the tiny village, the almost perfect circle of ancient stones was, in reality, constructed by Megalithic peoples over 4,000 years ago. Like so many other Megalithic sites throughout Great Britain, archaeologists today can only theorize about the true purpose of the circle.

When Andy, Janet and Graham arrived at the Rollright Stones on that warm Sunday afternoon, they were only concerned with the latter day usage of this site. Standing beside a narrow country road the stone circle is on privately owned property and a trust has been set up to ensure its preservation. The circle is open to the public and a small hut stands just inside a clump of nearby trees from where the wardens collect an entrance fee and maintain a protective watch over the circle. However, as they quickly discovered, there is nothing but simple goodwill to prevent anyone from entering the circle at the dead of night. As darkness descends the stones are left alone, a timeless monument to the ancients who erected them.(1)

As Andy and Janet made their way round the ring, attempting to defy the legend that the stones cannot be counted, Graham spoke to the woman in the hut, casually suggesting that he was interested in witchcraft being practised there.

'Well,' she said, 'it was a good few years ago now, back in the forties or fifties, I think. There was a lot of talk, and several people claim to have seen them.'

'Is there any evidence that it continued.'

'No, they seemed to give up after the police became interested. Tried to tie it up with a murder.'

'On Meon Hill?'

'You know about it then?'

Graham nodded.

'Someone wrote a book about it.' (2)

Unfortunately this hardly proved that witchcraft had been practised there since the 1950s. However from the adjoining road anyone could come and go as they pleased. As no houses stand anywhere near the circle and the road is little used, it was probable that no-one would be likely to know.

So how could they discover whether a coven practised there today? Had the 1940s/50s coven finally left the Rollrights after falling under suspicion for the savage murder of Charles Walton? Whoever they were they had not been arrested. Were the Meon Hill murderers, or at least their successors, about to return to the Rollright Stones as Marion had suggested?

About four hundred yards to the south-east of the circle stand the Whispering Knights, a group of five megaliths thought to have been the remains of an old burial chamber contemporary with the Rollright Stones. In legend the five men were also petrified as they knelt together, plotting and scheming some distance from the King and his main band of men. As they drew nearer they saw that one of the stones lay horizontal, fallen centuries ago to give the Whispering Knights the appearance of huge vultures gloating over a stony carcass lying between them.

As Andy looked over the iron railings surrounding the stones his jaw dropped. Janet had seen it first. Graham stared blankly. On the recumbent stone, as if on a sacrificial altar, lay what at first looked like a posy of tiny red flowers. A closer examination revealed they were not flowers but red and black berries woven into a ring large enough to wear as a head band. Berries, twigs and thorns interwoven together.

★   ★   ★   ★

So someone with a knowledge of witchcraft had been there, and recently too. It was almost certain that the stones were being made ready for a witchcraft ceremony. They did not touch or remove the entwined ring, deciding it was best to leave it undisturbed.

Halloween was just three days away. Perhaps someone would return that night to continue their magical preparations. They, too, would return secretly to keep watch. They booked into the White Hart hotel at Moreton-in-the-Marsh and Andy telephoned the others before they prepared to set off to the Rollrights. They thought it sensible to notify someone else of their intentions.

Marion's voice was almost deafening as she answered the phone.

'Where are you?' she cried.

'Near the Rollright Stones,' he answered.

'You must get away from there,' she urged. 'Gaynor's been frantic all day. She's certain you're in great danger. You must get away now!'

She told them of Gaynor's vision in the church that morning, of the woman and the ring of berries. The accuracy was unbelievable. They decided there and then to cancel the hotel reservation and leave immediately. But this was not all. Marion insisted they must not return to Wolverhampton, but go directly to her house. They could stay the night. Whatever happened they must come. She was insistent.

They drove the 150 miles to Flint, arriving in the late evening. What might have happened had they returned to the Rollright Stones would never be known. They could only guess what their phone call to Marion Sunderland might have saved them from.

On the morning of Monday, 29 October, Andy and Graham returned to Knights Pool with Janet, Marion and Gaynor. It was their first sight of the lake in daylight, and they were eager to photograph the bridge and, if possible, to discover more about its history. The lake lies on the estate of nearby Croome Court, which was once the stately home of the Earl of Coventry, but today is owned by the Society for Krishna Consciousness as their British headquarters and as a meditation centre.

Gaynor felt intuitively that they must return to the pool. The previous evening she had said that at last she knew the purpose of the sword, and the answer to its hidden secret. It was not the cryptic message that was important but the sword itself which would lead them to the Stone. She insisted that she personally must take the sword to the bridge. This was why she had been shown the bridge and the running man in her dream.

In the light of day Knights Pool was not nearly so sinister as its cold waters had been at the dead of night. Water fowl swam across the pool, occasionally diving for food in the murky depths. A soft breeze blew through the surrounding trees, as the autumn leaves fell on to the quiet waters.

As Gaynor stood above the bridge staring quietly across the pool, Andy and Graham explained to Janet and Marion how they had uncovered the sword. Gaynor was deep in thought. After a while she asked for the sword. She took the hilt in both hands and stretched out her arms. Slowly and deliberately she began to turn, pointing the sword slightly into the air before her. She stopped. The sword pointed away from the lake in the direction of a small apple orchard that lay just beyond the wood.

'Over there,' she said. 'About a mile away there's an old ruin. We must go there now.'

Marion expressed no surprise. But the other three stared at Gaynor who smiled back and shrugged nonchalantly. How she knew she could not say, but she insisted she was right.

'That's it,' exclaimed Marion, as Gaynor handed the sword back to Andy. 'The feeling I had the other day about the secret of the sword being different to what we thought.' It seemed that Gaynor was to use the sword itself to locate the Stone. But there was more to the sword than a simple divining rod. It would not lead directly to the Meonia Stone.

They followed the bearing she had been given. Just beside the road, a mile or so to the south-east of Knights Pool, stood the remains of an old castle. The decaying building looked like an ancient gothic gatehouse, its once great but now crumbling arch spanned the battlemented wall linking two of the surviving turrets.

Gaynor stared at one of the towers, oblivious of the young girl riding towards them. Marion, however, watched the girl as she approached, a curious expression of recognition on her face. As the girl pulled up her horse Gaynor still stared up at the tower. Marion spoke to the girl as Graham, Andy and Janet investigated the old ruins.

When the child had gone Marion explained that she had asked her about the ruins. The girl had said that it was only a mock castle, built in the late 18th century at the whim of a local Lord.

Graham shook his head. 'If it's only that old then the Stone can't be here.'

'No, it's not,' answered Marion, 'but something else is.' She turned and cast a final glance toward the young girl riding into the distance.

'Gaynor's been led here, I don't know how or why, but something is here, something we need to know.'

'You seem very sure,' said Graham.

'I am, because of that girl on the horse. Remember what I said about a white horse, just before I saw the avenue of trees? I'm certain that was a premonition, and the girl convinces me that our answer lies here.'

Gaynor suddenly announced that she must go inside the tower. The one tower still stood in its entirety, a doorway in the side about six feet above ground level. They could gain access through a narrow opening, where some of the planks used to board it up had been torn away. Marion said the building looked unsafe, but Gaynor insisted. Eventually Graham, being the tallest, agreed to climb in and examine the interior.

It was dark inside; the only light came in from the opening through which he peered. As his eyes adjusted to the darkness he was able to distinguish the first steps of the stone stairway that wound its way high into the tower. It looked sturdy enough. He squeezed through the opening, the musty air filling his nostrils. Gaynor and Andy joined him.

Between the outer and inner walls surrounding the stairway they peered up into the tower, their fading torch lighting only a few feet. They could see nothing of what lay above in the darkness.

But it was there that Gaynor felt her answer lay. Graham went first, following the spiralling steps, leading the way with his torch to ensure it was safe. Gaynor followed close behind. Andy remained behind to relay any messages to Janet and Marion outside.

They had half ascended the tower when there came a strange crashing from above. Graham froze. He turned to face Gaynor. She was calm, unmoved by the noise overhead.

She wanted to go on. She knew her answer was above. An oppressive silence fell in the tower. They went on. The noise came again, louder and more prolonged, a rough scraping resounding through the darkness, followed by dull powerful thuds. There was something up there. It was no natural crumbling of masonry.

'We're coming down,' shouted Graham. Another loud report filled the air. 'Come on, Gaynor,' he ordered. Reluctantly, she agreed. They turned and began the descent.

The sounds grew louder, like the agitated flapping of wings.

'What the hell is it?' Andy called out.

'I don't know, but it's damned big,' came Graham's reply. There was a loud thud as a huge chunk of stone crashed down from above, smashing to pieces only inches from were Andy stood. Graham and Gaynor appeared round the foot of the stairs, rubble and dust falling behind them.

For a while they waited in the safety of the sunshine outside. They were sure it had been a bird, a large bird. But what bird could have shifted so much debris? An owl or a buzzard? No, whatever it was it was much larger.

As they drove away Gaynor sat deep in thought. She had not been led to the tower for nothing. Something had been waiting there for her. Had they allowed her she would have seen it. She knew now that it would come to *her*.

The night of Halloween was only two days away. Joanna had said they must find the Meonia Stone by that day, but what would happen if they failed? Marion was now convinced that the dark-haired woman and her witch coven would meet at the Rollright Stones on the night of Halloween, and everyone who had received psychic impressions felt that the evil force which operated through her would be free to wreak irrevocable havoc if the Stone was not found.

They could not help but remember the uncanny accuracy of so many of the other psychic messages. There was growing concern and anxiety. Their hopes had been dashed. For a moment they had thought that Gaynor was about to locate the Stone, since she had been so accurate about the ruined castle. Now they were still no nearer.

Both Gaynor and Marion believed that the sword itself would lead them to the Stone. Instead, it had led them to a ruin which was not nearly old enough.

'We're forgetting Pakington logic,' said Andy, when they arrived back in Oakenholt. 'Perhaps we ought to think again, and reason it out logically as we did before.'

It was then that Fred Sunderland made a constructive suggestion, after he had tucked Gaynor safely in bed. They should re-examine

the map, and search for a possible name association. This had led
them to the sword, so why not to the Stone. But where to look? He
reminded them of Gaynor's dream of the running man. She felt that
he had already hidden something before making for the bridge, so
surely that dream could help. They all agreed. But first they must
find out from where he had originally come. It was almost certainly
Huddington Court, since it lay only about nine miles from the pool,
considerably nearer than Harvington Hall. The haste of Gaynor's
runner and the torrential weather conditions also indicated that the
Stone had been hidden almost immediately.

Fred drew a straight line between Huddington Court and Knights
Pool. He then pencilled a broad ellipse between the two.

'I think we can be pretty sure it's in this area,' he said.

'It's still too big,' Graham observed.

'Then lets narrow it down,' he said, and went on to recall more
details of Gaynor's dream. When she had first seen him the man had
stumbled across some marshy ground.

'Low ground. What about a river basin?'

Two major river systems crossed the pencilled area, the Avon and
the Severn. They quickly discounted the latter. It was relatively
straight and no marshy land was indicated. Secondly, the runner in
Gaynor's dream would have had to double back, highly unlikely
considering his haste. However, the Avon meanders its way in a
south-westerly direction, passing through their ellipse with
marshes shown on both banks. If Fred was right, somewhere along
that short stretch of the river lay the Meonia Stone.

They scanned the area and found something that struck a chord, a
great bend in the river near the village of Birlingham marked the
Swan's Neck. Marion was sure she remembered reading about
Mary Queen of Scots having been referred to as the Swan, as a code
name, she recalled. Whether or not this was correct there is much to
link the swan with Rosicrucian lore, enough to have made the
symbol of the swan a central importance to mystics and
Rosicrucians in the year 1605 when the Stone was hidden.

The swan has long been a symbol for occultists, alchemists, magicians and mystics alike, signifying spiritual purity and power; the
power to overcome evil. (3) But why was the swan so important in
1605?

The year before, when the new star had appeared in the constell-

95

ation of Cygnus, the swan, taken both by astrologers and mystics to be a sign heralding political and religious changes, many had believed that it signified the birth of a New Age. In the Rosicrucian *Confessio* of 1615, this is mentioned with the other star that appeared in that same year in the constellation of Serpentarius, the snake, saying:

New stars, which do appear and are seen in the firmament in Serpentarius and Cygnus which signify and give themselves known to everyone, that they are powerful signs of great weighty matters. (4)

It appeared that Catesby would not have had the Stone were it not for the Rosicrucians wishing to enthrone the Princess Elizabeth. So the swan was of considerable importance to the Rosicrucians. Pakington logic therefore made the Swan's Neck a likely location.

Gaynor returned, as she knew she would. Once again she climbed into the old tower. This time she would know what awaited her at the top of the winding stairway. Graham again led the way into the darkness. Then came the noise, this time louder, more fierce, the beating of huge wings. Graham urged her to flee. As before they turned and ran, repeating the scenario. As they emerged into the moonlight she turned and gazed. The high tower loomed above her. From the top a great white swan launched itself into sky. Then Gaynor saw what she had come to see. Around its long, graceful neck hung a leather pouch tied by a cord. She knew the pouch contained the small green Stone.

She awoke as the dawn was breaking, knowing that the Stone lay about the swan's neck. But what did it mean?

Far away in the Wolverhampton flat Graham also awoke. He sat up in bed and looked around. What was it? Something was on his mind, something important he couldn't quite remember. It was just after 6 a.m. He had slept only a short time, but he was wide awake. For some unknown reason he was now *sure* that the Meonia Stone was hidden at the Swan's Neck. But that was not all. He felt a sense of urgency, something almost telling him that he could not afford to wait. Was it impatience or intuition that made him decide to dress and leave there and then, or *was* something urging him on?

He woke Andy, but decided it was unfair to ask him to get out of bed at that early hour. He told him that he intended to drive across to the Worcester Records Library to find out something more about the Swan's Neck.

Alan Beard was awakened by the telephone. The image he had seen in his dream was still vivid in his mind. The green Stone again, only this time inside a brass casket buried beneath the earth. But where? And only one day left.

Marion apologised for disturbing him so early, but it was most important. She explained what they had worked out the previous evening, and informed him that Gaynor had just told her about her new dream. She said that Gaynor had drawn a picture of a casket which she believed contained the Stone, a casket that she thought was made of brass. Realising that Gaynor's description of the casket matched the one in Alan's dream, they agreed it would be wise to check it out. Marion had already phoned Andy, who said he would contact the others and ask them to meet at the flat. They must be getting close; not only Gaynor and Alan but Terry also had received a psychic vision of the brass casket. Alan decided to join them and take the day off work.

★　★　★　★

Graham arrived in the Worcestershire village of Birlingham, which lies four and a half miles to the south east of Knights Pool. His map indicated a narrow farm track leading from the village to the River Avon and the Swan's Neck a few hundred yards distant. He needed to discover something about the area from the local farmer, who told him that the large bend in the river had been called the Swan's Neck for many years, and the land on either side was common land where summer tourists sometimes moored their boats. So there was nothing to stop him scouting around and digging if necessary. The farmer added that there were no old bridges or ancient monuments in the vicinity.

Graham thanked him and set off along the dirt track leading to the Swan's Neck. Soon he came to a bend in the muddy path, finding himself in a small wood beside the river. Here the slow-moving water meandered through grazing land and small wooded copses, until it came through the great bend called the Swan's Neck, where he stood between the weeping willows that hung down onto the reeds at the river's edge. He was on the outside bank of the meander, looking over to the opposite bank which was bereft of trees. That side was almost an island created by the loop in the river and he could see why the impressive meander had earned its name.

He looked around in dismay. Even if the Meonia Stone was buried here, where on earth could it be? It would be an almost impossible task, the area of land around the Swan's Neck was simply too large.

In any case he was probably on the wrong side of the river. Pakington logic told him that the other side was a more feasible location. He would probably have buried the Stone somewhere in the centre of the loop on that side. Even if this was correct, they would still have a terrific job finding the exact centre. Besides, how deep would they have to dig?

He was about to leave when he turned and noticed the trees behind him. Alongside the Swan's Neck was an avenue of trees, between which ran the remains of an old cart track. The avenue was exactly as Marion had described when she had 'seen' where the Stone was hidden. She must have been right. The Stone was there somewhere. *It had to be.*

He paced back and forth along the avenue reasoning that obviously it would not have been there in Pakington's time, yet Marion had somehow seen it in her vision So she must have seen it as it stands today.

Suddenly he was struck by an intriguing possibility. If Marion *had* mentally projected to where the Stone lay, then it might follow that she was describing the avenue of trees from the position where she had been standing. If he could discover the spot then he would know approximately where the Stone was buried.

Marion had looked along a nearby avenue of trees. *Nearby.* So she was not among the trees. But where? He moved around, seeking to look down the avenue from any position other than between it. The only view that tallied accurately with her description was from the end nearest the cart track, the opposite end being blocked by trees and a tall hedge. And besides, this end took him away from the Swan's Neck itself. The position from which he could clearly see placed him in the grassy pastures right next to the river.

Perhaps he was now in the approximate location. But it was still possible to walk many yards to either side, and a considerable distance along the line of sight, having a clear view down the avenue. There was only one thing to do. He would have to fetch Marion.

As he reached the car, fully intending to drive away, a strange sensation overcame him, the feeling that something was telling him, urging and pleading with him to go back. He tried to ignore it, but it grew stronger. How would going back help? Again something told him, he *could* find the Stone. He would know. Surely this was ludicrous. Marion had seen the avenue of trees, so she should be the one.

He decided to relent. He would return, although he still believed it was his imagination. A most unpleasant feeling of urgency stayed with him. It grew stronger, as if he were being told that time was running out. Something was telling him that their adversaries were at that very moment on the point of finding the Stone, coming for it at the Swan's Neck. Quickly he fetched his spade and trowel, again pacing along the bank from where Marion had seen the avenue. His mind raced. Where the hell was it? Minutes passed as he ran out of ideas. What to do? Where to dig?

He leant resignedly against one of two lone trees and again looked down the avenue. He would have to give up and fetch Marion. No, that would be too late. The feeling was overpowering. He turned and saw a slight rise in the earth, a low grass incline.

And then he *knew*. This was where he had to dig.

Gaynor knew. She knew where they would find the Meonia Stone, and what they must do. But she also felt the danger. Inside the brass casket they would find two stones. They must touch neither. The second stone was for protection, a guardian. To touch it meant death. To touch the Meonia stone would mean that the opposition would know it had been found. Not until the last possible moment would it be safe to touch it. Not only would they know, but they would also be able to trace it.

Marion lost no time. Now only too familiar with the accuracy of the psychic messages, she telephoned the Wolverhampton flat where Janet, Alan and Terry had met Andy and were awaiting a call from Graham before they set off for the Swan's Neck. She told them of Gaynor's message. The Stone was *buried* at the Swan's Neck. When they arrived they would know where to dig, but when they found the brass casket containing the Stone they must touch nothing inside. She suggested that they did not open it until Gaynor saw it.

Marion replaced the receiver.

They decided to wait a little longer until Graham telephoned to arrange a *rendezvous*.

★ ★ ★ ★

Graham had dug two holes, but each time he felt he was in the wrong place. Now he was certain. He dug almost frantically, continually glancing round as the feeling mounted that someone else was drawing ever nearer. Then his trowel hit something. A large stone? As he dug he could feel its shape. Too uniform to be a stone or rock. The trowel struck again. It felt like metal, something hollow. Whatever it was, he had found a man-made object. Digging deeper into the black earth he saw the object, a rectangular box.

He pulled the box into the daylight, finding it thick with mud and heavy for its size. It was about eight inches long, five inches deep and five inches wide.

His mind reeled. Could this be it? *Did the Meonia Stone actually lie inside this box?* He dared not think. His stomach was heavy with tense expectancy. He had to know. His hands trembled.

The deposits came away fairly easily and he found the box covered in a black resin. Beneath it he saw the dull sheen of the metal. As he feverishly picked away the remaining deposits he revealed a humped lid. He took his penknife and prized it between the lid and the main body, twisting and turning, breaking the seal that must have held it together for so many years. With a final twist it came open. Inside was a small silver box about three inches square, adorned with a simple criss-cross design.

It opened easily. A shudder ran through him as he beheld the small *green stone*: The Meonia Stone. It was unreal. A dream! He stared in disbelief, stunned and shocked, unable to accept what he saw. The only thing his shocked senses registered was the simple, half egg-shaped Stone. He sat on the grass, shaking his head while he continued to stare.

Good God! The Meonia Stone really existed. Small, only three-quarters of an inch long and half an inch wide, a stone passed through time from an Egyptian Pharoah, to Gwevaraugh the Iron Age Queen, to the Knights Templar, the Rosicrucians and the Gunpowder Plotters. And now to them. What power could such a simple jewel hold? It looked so ordinary, a two-tone shade of pale sea green.

He moved to pick it up, but something stopped him. He must not touch it. It was wrong, very wrong. He quickly pulled back his hand as if he had been burnt. Then he noticed something else. In a corner of the casket was a small, black rectangular object, about an inch long, half an inch wide and deep. He moved to touch it. Again he was stopped. Under no circumstances must he touch it.

The sense of urgency punched his mind back to reality. He must leave. The impression was so powerful that he broke into a cold sweat. Then a sudden calm flowed through him. The urgency was still there, but he was calm. Everything seemed unreal. He must throw away the black object, throw it in the river. But he must not touch it. He took the trowel and with it lifted the metal or stone object, and walked slowly to the bank of the river, arm outstretched. He lifted the trowel and tossed the black object high into the air. It arched silently and fell into the waters, to be lost forever in the murky depths of the river.

He hurried back to the car, slid the Stone into a paper bag, the only container he could find, and put it in one of his trouser pockets. For an inexplicable reason he returned to the hole and re-buried the empty silver box, filling the hole along with the others he had dug, and stamping the turf back into place. Even as he did this he did not know why. But it must be something to do with the opposition; they must not know he had found the Stone. They were coming, and they knew where to find it. Surely they would not be deceived with just a small silver box? They would know for certain that it had not been on its own. It would have no deposits covering it. And they would be able to tell that holes had already been dug. He had an answer, but could make no good sense of it, although it had something to do with leading them astray, into believing that a third party had found the Stone.

As he ran back to the car a further impression struck him. He must tell no-one that the Stone had been found. He must return with the others to the Swan's Neck as if nothing had happened. Only he must know. When they reached the safety of Marion's home he must give the Stone to Gaynor, before he or anyone could touch it. Why could he not take it to her now, immediately? The answer was a definite no. He jumped into the car and drove away.

Safely out of the area he pulled into a lay-by. In his pocket lay the Stone. He was sure now that the opposition was real. But it was not so much the witches that worried him. It was the evil force itself, whatever it was, which was his primary concern. A force that knew no distance or boundaries. His only hope was that it did not know he had the Stone. He was scared. The almost unreal experience at the Swan's Neck had passed. He was alone. He would feel safer with people around.

He sat in a small cafe in the nearby town of Pershore, trying to understand why he had experienced such a strong compulsion not to take the Stone to Gaynor straight away? Perhaps the opposition knew and were observing them. If so, why had they not stopped him? He could not solve the problem. Perhaps they could mind read. All he knew was that he must go through with it, and pretend the Stone had not been found.

When he telephoned the headquarters he discovered that they were all there, anxiously awaiting his call. He said he had been researching at the library. For convenience sake they arranged to *rendezvous* at Knights Pool before going on to the Swan's Neck. As he waited he cleaned the casket. Perhaps there was an inscription on it as there had been on the sword? The deposits came away relatively easily, revealing the box whole, not grey as he had first thought, but gold coloured. He examined it closely. It was brass, but without any inscription.

Shortly after lunch they met together at Knights Pool. Graham had by this time begun to doubt his feelings. Should he, after all, tell them so that they could go immediately to Marion's and escape from the area. But when they told him of Gaynor, Alan and Terry's visions of the casket, which were identical, and of Gaynor's impression of the two stones and of not touching the green stone until she had it, it confirmed his own impressions. He dare not ignore them.

They studied the O.S. map, deciding that the best side of the river to search first was the opposite bank to the Birlingham side. Graham remained silent. He decided to act as if nothing had happened. He must let them search.

As they left the narrow lane that leads to Knights Pool, Alan and Terry, following the others in Alan's car, noticed a white Ford Escort pulled out from a farm track opposite. It followed them at a steady pace, some distance behind. After several turnings it was still there. Terry and Alan glanced back nervously.

When they pulled up at the roadside to make a phone call to Marion the car passed them. Two men sat inside. Terry and Alan were relieved as it disappeared round a corner in the distance. They laughed. In the heat of the moment their imagination had got carried away. They set off again. As they rounded the corner they saw the car again, parked in an entrance to the left. It pulled out a couple of hundred yards behind them. After a short time it was gone once more. Again coincidence.

They pulled into a lay-by beside the road that looked down over the Avon and the Swan's Neck. Looking over the gate they could see the broad valley where the river follows its winding course into the plainly visible Swan's Neck, and the church tower in Birlingham rising above the trees. Climbing a gate, they set off down the pathway to The Swan's Neck. For some time they mulled round the area, unsure what to do next. Alan suddenly alerted them. On the hill where they had parked their cars was the white Escort. Two figures stood on the skyline, leaning over the gate. There was no doubt that they were being watched.

Graham was petrified. The opposition knew. His intuition had been right. How did they know? How had they known they would be at Knights Pool? Had they followed him there, and, if so, did they know he had the Stone?

They arrived back at the cars, relieved to find the Escort gone and their vehicles untouched. Graham breathed a sigh of relief, the brass casket, minus the Stone, had been hidden in the tool box in the boot of his car. Now he *must* keep up the charade, for everyone's safety.

They drove on, having decided to try the other side of the river, splitting into two groups to foil their adversaries. Alan and Terry parked by a bridge half-a-mile downstream from the Swan's Neck and walked along the river bank. Andy, Graham and Janet drove into Birlingham. When they joined up at the Swan's Neck, neither group had seen the white Escort again.

Everyone but Graham was astonished to find the avenue of trees as Marion had described. Excited by the discovery they began to search. Graham was now even more concerned. He knew the opposition were there watching and waiting. Suddenly Andy called them. He had found holes, evidence that someone had been digging.

Graham was terrified. A number of deep holes had been dug precisely where he had been. But he had refilled the holes he had made. There was no doubt, someone had dug in exactly the same spot during the two hours since he had left to meet the others. Perhaps they thought the grassy rise the most likely place, or had they seen him digging? If so, it might well mean trouble. They would know he had the Stone. Then why had they not tried to take it from him? Perhaps they were waiting for others and were ready to use force.

His dilemma was frightening. The very lives of his friends might hang in the balance. His only chance was to maintain the charade.

Much to his relief, Alan announced that he was sure he would know if the Stone had been found by the opposition. But he was confident they had not found it. Terry agreed. Andy and Janet dug in and around the holes, as Graham listened to Terry and Alan discussing their course of action. They all agreed they were probably being watched. What would they do, therefore, if they did find the Stone? As Terry and Alan continued their discussion, Graham joined Andy and Janet still digging around the holes. He could see clearly that the spot where he had reburied the silver box had been dug over. The silver box had undoubtedly gone.

Their search continued around the avenue of trees. Graham tried to stay calm. If they were under observation in that isolated setting there was trouble ahead. It was like waiting for a death sentence. As the light began to fade Graham decided they could wait no longer. There would be nothing suspicious about leaving as darkness approached; without light they could do little more.

But it was difficult to persuade them to leave. If necessary they were prepared to dig all night, believing there was still a chance of finding the Stone. Finally, they agreed to leave. On the telephone to

Wales Marion could tell them nothing more; she advised them to make for her house as soon as possible. At midnight the witches would begin their ceremony and it was better that they were together, with or without the Stone.

As they left Graham glanced round nervously, every second expecting a car to pull out and stop them. But there was nobody. They drove on through the night, each mile taking them nearer to North Wales and safety. Nothing happened. With each passing minute he felt more secure. He tried to reason out what had occurred, where the two men in the Escort had gone and how many more there might be.

At last they arrived. As the others went into the house he took the Stone and slid it from the bag back into the casket. He put it in his briefcase and followed them inside. He knew he must give the Stone to Gaynor, for she would know what to do with it. He asked Marion if he could speak to Gaynor but she said that she was already in bed. He told her it was important, so she went to check. They found her waiting at the top of the stairs.

'You've got something for me,' she said.

He opened the briefcase and removed the casket, handing it to her. Marion was open-mouthed. Gaynor smiled, and opened the box and looked inside. Not a flicker of surprise crossed her face.

Marion was almost speechless. 'Is that it?' she stammered. 'How did you ...?'

Graham hardly heard her. He glanced at Gaynor and then at the Stone.

'Yes,' he said, 'that's it.'

Marion burst into tears, 'Oh, my God, if we hadn't got it,' she cried.

They made their way downstairs.

As Graham explained, Gaynor said nothing. She sat and stared at the Stone. Still she did not touch it. When he had finished they looked to her for an answer. She had been so accurate before. The Swan's Neck, the two stones, the brass casket. They examined her drawing of the casket. It was identical. She had known Graham had it, so surely she must now know what happened next. She leant forward and picked up the green jewel. Then she handed the Stone to her mother.

'You must use it,' she said. They looked at her again. With a little

105

smile she turned and was gone, off back to bed. Her work was done.

In just under two hours the dark ceremony at the Rollright Stones would begin.

★ ★ ★ ★

At midnight, as they passed the Stone round, they all felt a strange vibration coming from it, a sensation almost of warmth. Marion took the Stone. She now knew what had to be done, although she could not explain it to the others. As she held the Meonia Stone in her hand she felt it almost growing, pulsating with energy.

She felt a mysterious sensation as she lay back in her chair. All she wanted to do was close her eyes. To sleep. She told them to sit round her in a semi-circle and remain quiet.

She was no longer in the room. The Stone seemed to vibrate. She felt a cold biting wind on her face. Then there was darkness. She was standing among trees, and she could hear the wind through their leaves.

Then she heard voices, chanting voices. Next the fire, crackling in the night. Burning wood, the heavy smoke. She saw them, a huge circle of grey-robed and hooded figures about the fire, inside the ring of stones. The flames cast long shadows around them. A single black-robed figure stepped forward to the fire, a woman with long black hair. It was she. The leader.

The woman threw back her arms and head, shouting aloud into the night. The coven responded. She chanted again, reaching out, stretching and clawing at the sky like a cat.

Light. A sickly orange light tore away the darkness above her. She shrieked in ecstasy. The coven chanted in response.

Marion knew that the force of pure evil would manifest through the woman in physical form. She felt the Stone pulsating, throbbing in her hand. A shape began to form in the orange light, a huge winged mass. Then came a cry, a cry of triumph from the manifestation. The woman screamed, her cries merging with the demon's.

The Stone burned into Marion's hand. She had to stop it. *Use* the Stone. She felt the power growing within her, her spirit body overflowing with energy. Concentrating her entire force of will against the fiery abomination she felt an immense shock jar her body. It was

106

turning on her. There followed a brief moment of struggle. It was too powerful. It could overcome all that was directed towards it. She knew she could not destroy the evil by force, it thrived on such actions. She must return its *own* malefic intent. *Use the Stone to reflect its power.* Light burst round Marion as she held the Stone before her. The abomination recoiled. Enveloped in an intense whiteness it gave a final embittered cry and was gone. The woman sank to her knees, bathed in white light. Then she ran in terror. The power of the witch coven and their priestess was at last broken. The demon was gone.

Marion woke from the strange sleep and blinked up at them. She relaxed and smiled.

'It's all over,' she said, sighing with exhaustion. 'We have done it. We've won. Now we can rest.'

The force had lost its power over the Warwickshire Coven. (5) That night they all believed the evil had finally been destroyed. But, in reality, it had lost only the first battle. Now it had an advantage, for at last it was aware of its opponents.

Chapter Eleven

A Sense of Evil

THE impossible had happened. They had found the Stone. From that day onwards their lives would never be the same again.

But what *was* the Meonia Stone and what were its origins. All they knew was what Joanna had told them, that it was a Stone that could be used to overcome this unnamed force of evil.

It had been closely guarded by a select few for centuries. It had come from the Megalithic culture of Britain, a race whose monuments still survive today in the form of standing stones, stone circles, long barrows and burial chambers scattered throughout the British Isles. The Pharoah Akhenaten had fallen heir to the esoteric knowledge possessed by these peoples, a knowledge which had ultimately led to their destruction. It had been created to oppose the evil force which had eventually destroyed them. But this was all they knew. Could Joanna be contacted again?

Graham made further unsuccessful attempts to fall into the trance state to enable them to communicate with Joanna. Still she would not return to help them.

Yet it was not from Joanna that they were to find their answer. It was from Gaynor and another child, a teenager called Andrew James who had first contacted Marion after she had appeared in the local newspaper requesting other UFO witnesses to come forward and report their experiences.

In the summer of 1976 Andrew had been walking along Coed-on lane, the same lane from which Gaynor had seen her UFO. The narrow road begins on the outskirts of one of the Oakenholt housing estates, and leads to a number of farms in the surrounding districts. Where it leaves the estate it overlooks the Oakenholt school. As he walked down the lane that summer afternoon, he became aware of a bright multicoloured object above the school. He watched as it manoeuvred, banking towards him and after further manoeuveres disappearing in the distance. In the windows in the side of the object he had seen several figures looking down at him.

Although he was unable to recall the exact date, he was sure the experience had occurred within a week or so of Gaynor's in July. Andy, Graham and Martin had questioned him closely and found his testimony consistent. In addition, many of the circumstances tallied with certain unpublished details of close-encounter cases they had been investigating.

In the weeks and months following this encounter, Andrew was to develop quite remarkable ESP. He, too, appeared to have maintained psychic contact with the beings inside the craft.

During November 1979, Gaynor and Andrew, simultaneously and quite independently of one another, both felt inspired to make a number of drawings and automatic writings concerning the Megalithic culture. (1) Neither of them knew anything of the involvement of the Megalithic people with the Stone. For unexplained reasons, they both felt inspired to make drawings of standing stones and stone circles, burial mounds and chambered tombs.

The writings spoke of a great power that Megalithic people controlled, a power that could be harnessed at certain selected sites on the earth, to enhance what we would today call psychic abilities. But most interesting of all was a series of drawings made by Gaynor, which appeared to represent a pictorial history of the Megalithic civilization. The last picture was a representation of the Meonia Stone at the centre of a stone circle on an altar. Gaynor said that the Stone itself had been used by Akhenaten's followers who came to Britain to oppose the evil force that had helped bring about the downfall of the Megalithic civilization.

If the Meonia Stone had existed for so long was there any historical reference to it? Surely there must be a legend. Andy discovered several legends concerning a small green stone that allegedly held great power, and about a magical green gem that acted as a talisman against evil. (2)

The possibility that Marion's astral projection to the Rollright

Stones had been her imagination was dismissed when John Ward telephoned the Wolverhampton headquarters to report a dream he had experienced on the morning of Halloween. The dream was almost exactly as described by Marion, although he knew nothing of the witches coven that night at the circle.

As Alan set off for work on 1 November he experienced the most terrible feeling. By now he was becoming used to the psychic messages, but this time there was something different. The feeling was one of panic. Then he was sure. The opposition knew who they were and knew them all. Now it would begin its assault. First it would attempt to isolate them, to break up the group. He tried to shake off the feeling, to persuade himself it was only imagination. He had thought it was finished. They had found the Stone, and destroyed the evil. Surely their task had been completed. Andy, Graham and Terry could discover what it had all been about. All he wanted to do now was to rest and spend a few days at home with his wife and two small children.

Still he could not shake off the feeling, and when he arrived at work it grew even stronger. He felt the evil, too, a sense of something dark, brooding and unseen. No sooner did he become aware of it than it was gone, and as he forgot about it and pushed it to the back of his mind it would suddenly recur, each time more powerfully.

Later that morning one of the girls in the office looked at him stangely.

'These people,' she said, 'the people you're involved with. How well do you know them?'

Alan looked at her. What was she talking about? Marion, Terry and the others perhaps? This was not possible, the girl new nothing of his private life.

'Who d'you mean?' he asked.

'You know damn well,' she replied, staring him hard in the eyes. Suddenly her expression became more intense.

'They're evil. You must have nothing more to do with them.'

He was surprised and frightened. She was staring straight at him, her eyes blank and expressionless. What did she mean? How could she know? He suddenly remembered the warning, and the feeling he had earlier that morning. He knew she was being used.

'No. I don't believe that,' he said defiantly. Still her eyes pierced him. 'Who are you?' he stammered.

Her expression changed to a sardonic grin. She laughed.

'You don't think you will die yet, do you? Well, you will. You will die in a road accident.'

He was terrified, but said nothing.

Suddenly it was gone. The girl stared around her, a puzzled expression on her face as if she did not know where she was. She looked at Alan and smiled nervously, before returning to her work.

He immediately telephoned Marion and told her what had happened. The opposition was far from beaten.

'She was possessed. Marion, I'm scared. It's going to kill us all.'

She tried to calm him. Only that morning Gaynor had received a further psychic impression that no matter what happened they must remain calm. Evil fed on fear.

'I thought we had destroyed it,' he said.

On Monday, 5 November Andy and Graham were at the Wolverhampton headquarters with Andy's fellow investigator, Barry King, from London. He planned to stay overnight. A short time after midnight Barry suddenly complained of feeling very cold. He kept looking around, certain there was something in the room. He pointed to the metal bookshelves in one corner, indicating that the presence was there. There was a sudden huge crash on the metal, as if someone had struck it with a heavy hammer. Moments later there was a second loud crash.

Before the night was over Barry had decided to pack his case and leave.

A week or so later Terry and Alan had visited Marion, Gaynor and Fred to discuss their mounting fears and the strange sense of foreboding that had descended on the whole group. Something was about to happen, they could feel it slowly building in intensity.

As they drove home through the night Alan noticed something in his driving mirror. They turned and saw it, clear in the sky behind them. A strange light, far too large to be a star or planet. It was no

The Swan's Neck. The avenue of trees seen by Marion Sunderland in her psychic vision.

Martin Keatman at Avebury stone circle, where he and four others were surrounded by a strange blue aura of light.

Wayland's Smithy. Graham Phillips before the entrance to the chamber which held one of the Nine Lights.

Harvington Hall. A secret coded message made after the
Gunpowder Plot was hidden there, and remained unsolved
for almost four centuries.

Robert Wyntour, Squire
of Huddington. This is
the only surviving
portrait of any of the
Gunpowder conspira-
tors. It was Wyntour's
wife Gertrude who was
charged with the safe
keeping of the Meonia
Stone after the plot had
been discovered.

Humphrey Pakington. The man
responsible for hiding the Stone
and preparing the coded message
at Harvington Hall.

The ruined tower near Knights Pool that held a supernatural message for the team.

Jane McKenzie (L) and Pat Shotton before the temple at Biddulph Grange, the former home of Mary Heath.

The cellars beneath the Oaks Crescent headquarters, where an exorcism was attempted.

The brass casket and sword which held the clue to the stone's discovery.

The brass casket unearthed so dramatically beside The Swan's Neck on the River Avon.

White Ladies Priory. Terry and Alan looking towards the scene of the incredible psychic battle that took place on 1 February 1982.

Alan Beard (L) and Terry Shotton on the grassy mound known as the *Place of Darkness*.

Gaynor Sunderland on the bridge at Knights Pool where the sword was discovered.

Marion Sunderland and Mike Ratcliffe in the Sunderland family living room.

aircraft. They drove on, losing sight of it.

A few miles further on they saw it again, a huge red orange light pursuing them along the road. For miles it followed them, manoeuvering across the sky as they negotiated the dark bends along the deserted country road. At 1.00 a.m. there were no other cars on the road. No houses with comforting lights. They were alone. The light drew nearer. They were about to call in to a farmhouse and alert its occupants when the light banked away and disappeared. It was gone. They drove home, afraid that the mysterious ball of light would again return and pursue them. But it did not.

As winter progressed everyone felt the dark feeling growing upon them. Something dreadful was about to happen. Nearly all the psychics involved had overpowering impressions that something evil would soon befall one or all of them.

During the first week of December Terry and Alan visited Marion's again. Maybe they could find a method of communicating with whatever it was that seemed to help them, and perhaps discover the purpose behind the force opposing them. For weeks there had been silence, no psychic messages or impressions. As they sat in Marion's front room that night, Alan and Gaynor received simultaneous messages.

Alan heard a voice, saying: 'I am she that is with you.' Then they all had a strong impression that an unseen presence had entered the room. Marion and Gaynor admitted that they had sensed the same presence all day, but could not understand it. Alan seemed to be most in tune for he suddenly had a further impression of the words, 'the key to time and life,' enter his mind when the others asked him about the Stone.

Suddenly, a vivid image flashed through Gaynor's mind. Quickly she drew what she had seen, a grassy hill with a single oak tree near the top. She was sure that this was where their answer lay.

At that time they thought that the presence they had felt and who had given Alan the message, 'I am she that is with you', was, in fact, Joanna. They were sure they had to find her.

After several attempts Graham was able to fall back into the trance state. Joanna again spoke, warning that the evil force was beginning to use further people, but she refused to say more about their quest or the history of the Stone. However, she did eventually tell them who she was: a woman living in Cornwall, someone Graham had known in his college days.

Later, when he and Andy visited her at her home she was very surprised, but consciously knew nothing of any messages that she had given them. However, she said to Andy that she felt she had seen him before.

So what had spoken through Graham? Was it Joanna? They were forced to conclude that it was not, and that the intelligence that had led them to the Stone had simply used Joanna as a belief system that Graham's mind could accept, although he did not know why. Obviously it had no wish to reveal its true identity.

So who was *She that is with you?*

As the days passed the various psychics still felt that something was about to happen that might well destroy the group. The tension grew as days turned into weeks. It was the headquarters that appeared to be the focal point of the malevolence. Everyone who visited the flat felt a strange depression, a heavy, stifling feeling. Terry and Alan sensed it so greatly that they became increasingly reluctant to visit the place.

It was not long before light bulbs began to implode, one after the other, and the *malaise* continued to grow. No explanation was found.

Chapter Twelve

———————◆———————

Imbolc — Festival of Fear

*T*UESDAY *29 January 1980.* During the week leading up to Friday 1 February the Oaks Crescent flat became the focus of some of the strangest paranormal phenomena in the history of psychical research. It began with the strange electrical anomalies that had been occurring for some time becoming even more dangerous.

On a number of occasions both Andy and Graham received electric shocks from the cooker and the fridge. They were unable to account for these even after investigation.

Wednesday 30 January.

In the morning they examined the wiring in the kitchen, double checking for a fault or exposed wire that might account for the phenomena. They found nothing.

Later that day they were working on the precis for a proposed TV documentary. Andy was in the main office and Graham in the kitchen.

It was just before five thirty when the doorbell rang. Andy went to answer it but the drive was empty. No-one was in sight. He ran quickly to the end of the drive, searching for children who might be playing a prank on them. No-one. Most of the crescent can be seen from the driveway and it would therefore have been impossible for anyone to ring the bell and escape without being seen. He walked along the crescent, still half expecting to see the cheeky face of a small child peering at him from behind a wall. But the crescent was deserted. He returned to his work, still puzzled. Perhaps the wiring in the bell was faulty. He would need to check it.

115

A little later he joined Graham in the kitchen and over coffee they discussed their progress. Andy made to go back to the office, but as he opened the kitchen door into the hallway a mass of thick smoke billowed into the kitchen. He stepped back in shock.

'The place is on fire.' Graham shouted. The two men edged into the hallway. The long corridor was thick with dense smoke, but the smell was strange, something like a heavy, musty incense. They moved round the flat; all the rooms were full of the mysterious smoke. But there was no fire. Entering the front room they could hardly see from one end to the other, but found nothing to account for the phenomenon. The fire-place had not been used for days and there were no half-kindled ashes in the grate. Opening all the windows it took half-an-hour to clear. Then they telephoned Terry to tell him what had happened and to hurry over.

He arrived at six thirty and the three of them spent the next two and a half hours attempting to find a natural explanation for the smoke. At about nine o'clock Terry was about to leave. Then, as they opened the front door they saw an incredible sight. Stuck into the wood surround of the doorstep was a huge metal dagger.

'Bloody hell,' said Terry, recoiling in horror. The blade was at least ten inches long, and the dark brown wooden handle was bound with leather thongs topped by a metal cap.

Graham quickly scanned the dark crescent. There was no-one in sight. He knelt down and touched the hilt. Without a second thought he grasped it firmly and tugged. It was stuck firm. He tugged again, harder. The heavy-handled weapon came away in his hand. Quickly he retreated into the office, but Andy ran into the drive, any second expecting to see a dark shadow loom up before him. But the crescent was empty except for one person, a young man delivering leaflets from door to door.

Andy called him over and questioned him. He had been to the next door house only ten minutes earlier, and had seen the dagger in their step. So it had been there for at least ten minutes, so whoever was responsible must now be well clear.

Terry telephoned Marion, but before he had a chance to utter a word Marion had seen it. In her mind's eye she saw the ugly dark-grey blade about ten inches long, with a thong-bound handle and metal support.

'Don't *touch* it, whatever you do,' she said.

116

'It's too late,' said Terry, 'Graham and Andy already have.'

'Then you must bury it in salt. Quickly. Away from the house.'

'Why?' said Terry.

'*Do it,*' pleaded Marion. 'Now!'

Terry told Andy, who hurried to the kitchen to find the salt. He traced the dagger and measured it. The blade was ten and a half inches long. He grabbed his trowel and ran across the road into the dark shrubland opposite the crescent. Although in the town, one side of the crescent is a large wooded area, the ground surrounding what is now the local Water Authority headquarters. Andy dug. The trees swayed in the cold wind as he knelt on the wet soil. Every small sound jolted him. The wind in the trees. Small creatures scurrying through the undergrowth, snapping the dead branches and twigs beneath. He finished the hole and poured it full of salt, and with a last glance at the cold steel of the blade he placed it carefully onto the salt bed. He piled back the soil, thumping it down with the trowel and then his feet. With a last heavy stamp he had finished.

Marion was convinced it was a witchcraft dagger. The weapon was certainly hand-made, but was she correct? Was it really intended as a curse, or could it possibly have been a prank in bad taste? Andy decided that the best course was to telephone an acquaintance in London who was something of an authority on the occult. He would describe the dagger and see what he made of it.

When told he was very concerned. The dagger was a *burin*, a witchcraft knife used for carving effigies of potential victims. It appeared that the events they had been experiencing over the past few days, the exploding lightbulbs, unexplained electrical faults and incense-smelling smoke were a sure indication of what occultists call psychic attack, supernatural forces being deliberately brought to bear against an opponent. The dagger incident was almost certainly connected, although it seemed that this act was more of a threat than an essential part of the operation. An attempt to frighten the victim.

Unless they were mistaken, there was now no doubt that their adversary was making his move. It had perhaps manipulated some new earthly emissaries to prove it, to send final physical proof of its intentions. The battle was on. What its purpose was they hardly dared contemplate.

At ten o'clock Martin telephoned. Unlike Graham and Andy, who were able to work full-time on paranormal research, he had been

117

unable to accompany them on their recent investigations since he was employed by a civil engineering firm. He could hardly believe his ears.

Andy next phoned John Avis, the UFO abductee from Aveley in Essex. Like Gaynor, John had also claimed to have maintained contact with the aliens who had abducted him and his family. He suggested that they should all concentrate their psychic energies to repel the psychic attack being made upon them.

Terry had gone. Andy and Graham sat talking in the office. At ten thirty the smoke appeared again, but this time only in the hallway. They paced along it, searching for an answer, the smoke swirling about them as it slowly grew thicker. Still they could not discover from where it was coming. As it began to clear they returned from the corridor to the office. Andy left the connecting door partially ajar. Suddenly there was a resounding crash and the door slammed heavily into its frame behind him. Something in the corridor had smashed into the door and closed it. Andy grabbed the handle and pushed the door. It would not move. Graham helped and they shoved harder, finally opening it with considerable difficulty. The corridor was empty. Only the faint smell of the smoke remained.

Behind the door was a bundle of magazines, the weight of which had blocked it as they had tried to open it. Halfway down the twenty-foot-long corridor were several stacks of magazines in heavy bundles. Some unseen force must have thrown one of these bundles against the door and slammed it shut. Whatever it was, it had thrown the magazines a distance of at least six feet. As Andy moved forward the hallway light bulb imploded, leaving him in total darkness. The tension was growing. Poltergeist phenomena, yet another aspect of psychic attack. If this unseen hand could move a bundle of a hundred magazines weighing around thirty pounds, what might it throw next? More importantly, what else was it capable of doing?

Thursday 31 January

Pig was a tabby cat, who demanded constant feeding. They did not know the real name of their next door neighbour's pet, but Pig was apt enough. He would often wander in and out of the open door of the office as they worked, waiting to be fed.

That afternoon he jumped into the porchway as usual, his front paws on the step into the office. But something was wrong. His hackles lifted; his back arched as he stared into the front room. They were shocked. The cat stared fixedly at the middle of the room as it slowly backed away, its fur quivering, before turning quickly and dashing down the drive. They looked at one another. What had the cat seen in the room? Whatever it was it had terrified him.

Minutes later the second of the neighbour's cats approached, Mr. Greedy. It, too, paused in the doorway, stared into the room and fled. Again they looked at one another. *Something* was in the building.

Five thirty came. Andy arrived back from a visit to the town just before Graham. He opened the front door and entered the office. As he checked the stationery he had just purchased a faint smell brushed through his nostrils. He glanced around. The room slowly began to grow misty; the smoke again, only this time he was determined to find where it was coming from. He searched the room as it thickened, but was unable to locate the source. It was appearing uniformly throughout the office. He was scared. This time he was alone. He plucked up courage and searched the house, discovering that the smoke was only in the office.

Graham arrived to find the smoke forming in the office. He had arrived in time also to witness its strange mode of appearance, from no one point and uniformly throughout the room.

Andy telephoned various people and told them what had occurred with the cats earlier that day. All day Martin, Marion and another girl, Anne Banks, who had recently visited the flat, all felt dizziness, nausea and experienced strange headaches. Marion was very worried. She was sure that the events were building up, leading inevitably to a major crisis.

Friday, 1 February

Imbolc: One of the four main pivot points of the Celtic calender, one of four ancient fire festivals of the year and a day long believed to hold supernatural significance. February 1 was also one of the eight Grand Sabbats of the witch cult. The two men were concerned.

Investigators of the paranormal rather than witnesses to it, both were aware that their credibility as objective paranormal researchers would be called into question by such claims. They therefore endeavoured to find further witnesses in case the smoke appeared again or there were other paranormal events. Their story was too fantastic, too incredible, they felt, to be believed by fellow investigators.

That Friday afternoon, at five thirty, five people stood witness to the mysterious smoke as it duly appeared in the front room of the flat. Andy and Graham were joined by Dawn Westwood, a woman in her early thirties from a flat nearby, and Lesley Connolly, the girl living in the flat above. The estate agent for the flats was also present. The latter made a hasty retreat at the first sight of the mysterious smoke. Once more they were unable to account for the smoke's origin as it again flooded the room. The other witnesses watched dumbstruck.

Martin arrived at seven o'clock. Andy explained everything that had befallen them during that eventful week. Once more the three of them sought a logical explanation, but to no avail.

As they talked the clock struck seven thirty. Martin and Andy were sitting on the couch facing the fireplace. Graham was at his desk. For a reason he cannot now recall Martin looked up at the radio which was on the mantlepiece over the fire. As his eyes registered the set it was gone, arching into the air to the right as he looked at it. The radio flew upwards, arched over the stereo speaker next to it and crashed downwards, smashing into the record player, badly damaging the plastic lid.

The three quickly examined the mantlepiece. Could it have fallen and given the appearance of lifting into the air? Impossible. They had all seen it happening. Besides, the unit was split nearly in two by the force.

Quickly they decided to leave the flat and discuss the thing over some drinks. They left at eight thirty, leaving the office light switched on as a burglar deterrent. They stayed in the warmth of the pub lounge until eleven o'clock.

When they returned the crescent was dark and empty. A light breeze swept along it as they made their way back to the flat.

'My God,' said Martin, 'the light's off!'

They looked. The large bay window was in total darkness.

'The door.' said Andy.

The front door was wide open. Martin knew damn well he had closed it, for he had been the last to leave. There was no doubt about it — someone or something had broken into the house. Perhaps they were still inside?

The three men ran into the pitch black room. Martin flicked the light switch. Nothing! They ran from room to room, fearing at any moment an attack by intruders. They searched the place from top to bottom. It was in total darkness and empty. They tried the light switches in each room. None of them worked. Whoever had broken in had fused all the lights.

Whilst Andy and Graham found candles Martin phoned Marion. As he spoke to her she had the mental impression of two men, one tall with dark hair and a beard, the second of average height and clean shaven. She saw no more, but she was certain it was these who had broken in.

'Quick! Martin,' Andy shouted.

He dropped the receiver and ran to join Andy and Graham in the candle-lit hallway. The smoke was thick, swirling and spiralling through the corridor, a dense cloud of musty incense filling their throats. With the candles they searched again unsuccessfully for the source. As the smoke began to thin, Martin went back to the telephone and apologised to Marion for having dropped the mouthpiece while she was speaking. As they talked Andy again called out, this time more frantically than before. Again Martin dropped the receiver and ran into the hallway.

The flickering half light of the candles cast indistinct shadows on the white kitchen walls. The three men were huddled in the doorway, a solitary candle illuminating the table and cupboards in the kitchen. As usual, they had left their dinner plates on the table. Splattered all over the plates, the table and the formica surface of the cupboards were dark blue masses, amorphous forms of blue jelly, like jellyfish.

They edged forwards into the kitchen. Andy held the candle over the largest mass. Martin leant over and smelt it, but it was odourless.

'Better not touch it,' he said. 'It might be poisonous.'

They examined it with the candles, totally lost for a logical explanation. Graham and Andy continued to examine it while Martin hurriedly returned to the phone.

On hearing the news Marion was very disturbed. She told him they must leave the flat immediately or something terrible might happen. But they felt they could not possibly leave the scene of so baffling a mystery. Then, said Marion, if they must remain, they had better prepare themselves for the night ahead. They must draw a double circle of chalk on the floor and stay within it. They must also make a circle of salt around that. This would act as a psychic protection so long as they stayed inside which, she insisted, they must. She said they must also barricade the doors.

Hurriedly they did as she had said, and with a length of string and a piece of chalk scribed out the double circle on the brown carpeted floor of the office. Then they stood the couch on end to block the door, supporting it with chairs.

As they finished and Andy was placing the chalks on the mantlepiece he suddenly began beating frantically at the front of his coat. Martin smelt burning as he stood next to him. Andy's coat was on fire. The nearest candle was feet away. Quickly Andy beat out the flames. If this force could set light to a coat then it could just as easily set light to the whole flat. They hurried on with the protective measures.

Fortunately they had sleeping bags and lying within the circle they talked into the night. Somehow the force, whatever it was, had attacked them, sending emissaries to break into their headquarters. It had also used psychic attack, poltergeists, strange smoke and now one of them had come close to being seriously injured. They prayed that the circle was powerful enough against such concentrated assault.

All was quiet. The talking slowed as sleep overtook them. Three recumbent figures, cocooned in sleeping bags, encircled by a white chalk circle.

The flames licked high into the air, rapidly engulfing the sleeping bag. His body began to burn. In his half dream Graham saw them. A dream? It was no dream. *It was real*. He shot up from the floor.

'Andy!' he yelled. Martin sat up quicky. Huge flames engulfed Andy in his sleeping bag. He leapt from it beating his arms and then the bag, dowsing the flames. He ran to the kitchen, plunging his hands and arms under the cold water. How had it happened? The candles had been nowhere near him. The nearest, three or four feet away from where he lay, had somehow projected and fallen on him. Andy returned, his sleeping bag in rags. He was badly burnt, his thumb and index finger blistered. Quickly they returned to the circle and found another blanket for Andy to use with what remained of his sleeping bag.

Had it been a warning, this literal festival of fire on the night of the Grand Sabbat? (1)

The welcome light of day filled the room. Now, at last, they were able to fix the electrical system before telephoning Terry to tell him what had happened. Terry reported that throughout the previous evening his wife Pat had experienced an unnaturally sore throat. All night she had been terrified, and in some way she had connected it with something dreadful, convinced that the three of them had been in terrible danger.

That Saturday evening, Martin had to return home. On his arrival his mother, completely unaware of everything, told him how they had discovered something very strange indeed that morning. Snow had been falling on Staffordshire for some days. Martin's father had parked the car at the top of the driveway. In the morning he had found a set of footprints, in single column, leading from the house and coming to an abrupt halt just before the car. He had told his wife and although they examined the prints they were quite unable to account for them.

The coincidence was too great. Besides, his father was a complete sceptic. If he thought something was strange it certainly was.

Andy and Graham travelled to Marion's for the weekend. Gaynor, until then, had said nothing of the attack. Now she spoke. The evil force was using every means to destroy their power to use the Stone. If they were unable to halt it then they would fail. She suggested that everyone must concentrate on the Stone, symbolically channeling their energies through it to oppose their adversary by psychic means.

All those who had become involved agreed to do as she told them. At seven o'clock that Sunday night they sat for five minutes in their own homes concentrating their thoughts on the Stone, which Gaynor was holding. At five minutes past seven Gaynor handed the Stone to her mother, smiled and told her quite calmly that the psychic attack was over. Their adversary no longer had the means to subject them to such a terrifying ordeal.

By using the Stone, Marion had already succeeded in taking the power that enabled the Evil Force to use the witch coven. Never again could it use them. Now it had launched a psychic attack, using further living agents to break into the headquarters and stick the dagger in the door. Gaynor was certain that their having meditated on the Stone that weekend had finally destroyed its power to use and manipulate people. At least for the time being.

Quite how she had been capable of using the Stone in this way she could not, or would not, say.

Chapter Thirteen

———◆———

She That Is With You

THEY had been brought together by a power beyond their understanding. They had been led to discover a mysterious green stone and had been attacked by some unknown force of evil. But still they did not know why. Why them? Perhaps they would know if they could find out what had happened to those who had once possessed the Stone, and had fallen heirs to the secret knowledge of the Megalithic culture? *The Nine?* Had it all ended in the early seventeenth century after almost 3,000 years. Surely the loss of the Stone had not brought about the end of *The Nine.* The whispering voice speaking through Graham via Joanna had told them that the Stone had been hidden before, during the period between Gwevaraugh and the Knights Templar, yet the secret society continued. What had happened after the Gunpowder Plot. What became of *The Nine?*

They had already tried to trace the later history of the Rosicrucians in searching for an answer, but this had led nowhere. The original Rosicrucians could conceivably have been involved, but the groups claiming to be Rosicrucian which followed them would, in all likelihood, have had no connection with this mysterious and nameless society, *The Nine.* Like the Templars before them, they would probably have known nothing of the original intentions of their founders.

Perhaps after the fatal error of judgement leading to the Gunpowder Plot, and the loss of the Stone, the society had decided to disband.

Marion had spent many hours pondering these questions when an intense impression suddenly struck her. It was as powerful as any of

125

the other earlier psychic messages she had received, and it told her that the sword was not as old as they believed. It was not the original that had been hidden after the Gunpowder Plot. At first she could not accept this. Surely the sword must be the one hidden by Pakington and Gertrude Wyntour? Yet she could not shake off the impression. Eventually she decided to do something that, under the circumstances, the others had decided against.

On Monday, 3 March 1980, Marion took the sword and casket to the Grosvenor Museum in Chester. Dan Robinson, the assistant curator, was impressed. He had never before seen such a casket and was certain it was of medieval origin about 400-500 years old. However, Marion's message about the sword was confirmed when he said that it was in fact only about one hundred years old. The method of casting determined its age.

Trusting in her latest psychic impression, Marion felt sure that the original sword had been replaced with the one they now had. But why? And who had found the original? She was certain it had been replaced by the successors of those who had hidden it. This was logical. If it had been inadvertently discovered by anyone else, then a replacement would not have been made. In addition, the sword had enabled Gaynor to locate the tower where the strange experience with the swan had taken place. The sword itself must have contained a psychic message, forged into it in the late nineteenth century by a now forgotten process. This threw more light on the swan incident in the tower, which would not have existed in Pakington's day. Perhaps this was yet another form of incredible psychic tape recording made by *The Nine* in Victorian times, a powerful thought-image so strong that when released it created physical effects.

If Marion was correct, and *The Nine* had continued, why had *they* not located the Stone? After all, they had found the original sword. Marion felt that Graham had known where to dig since he had been able to 'tune in' with Gaynor when he had accompanied her into the tower. The tower and sword psychic messages had been left by *The Nine* in Victorian times, so clearly they knew of the Stone and its whereabouts.

It seemed unlikely that the Victorians had repossessed the Stone and later hidden it again. So why had they left the Stone hidden? Who were they and what had happened to them? When Marion told Gaynor of her discovery, the latter said she felt that something tragic had happened to them, which had brought about the final end of their Order.

On Wednesday, 28 May, they discovered the next piece in the jigsaw. Andy and Graham were at Marion's when Alan Beard arrived. While there he had the impression of a fishing village and an old house. He felt that something important had taken place there during Victorian times. Gaynor then explained how she had been experiencing a recurring dream which she felt was also connected. In the dream a group of people were fleeing, attempting to escape the country from what seemed to be the same village Alan had seen. One of them was stabbed, a second poisoned, and another two died in a tunnel cave in. She felt that the people had been corrupted by the power they possessed, and that the Order had divided in terror and chaos.

A new sword had then been forged, which contained the message, and it had been replaced in preparation for those who would be brought together.

But what had drawn them together in late 1979 and 1980 to continue the work of the disbanded Order? Whatever it was it knew about the location of the sword. Gaynor's dream of the running man and Alan's vision of the sword near a mill house proved that. It also appeared to know where the Stone had been.

But had Gaynor, in her dream of the runner, seen something taking place in Pakington's day or in the Victorian period? She could not say. All she was able to recall was that his clothes were strange, dirty and wet. Maybe the original sword had not been in the bridge foundations at Knights Pool. It had obviously been near Knights Pool because of the clues in the Nine Worthies depictions at Harvington, but perhaps in another building. It was unfortunate that they had been unable to discover the precise age of the bridge, otherwise they would have known if this was the case. Either way the message in the sword showed that whoever made it knew where the Stone was hidden. But also whatever was behind the psychic messages, impressions and visions had known of the whereabouts of the Stone.

It knew where the sword and the Stone were hidden, but did not lead them directly to them because of the opposition. It had wanted to be sure that both were safe.

So who or what was guiding them?

Who had Marion seen when she had the vision of the woman with agitated hands at the conference? Was it a *woman* who was guiding them? It seemed possible, because of Alan's words, 'I am she that is with you.' They had communicated with her via Joanna, and once through Marion. Their only clue was the *Meonia fore Marye* inscription on the sword. Was *she* this *Mary*? The sword inscription had been made in the late 19th century so *she* was unlikely to be Mary Queen of Scots. More likely a woman who had lived during the Victorian Era. But who had she been? (1)

Confirmation that their guide was a woman from the past came when Terry and Alan called on Penny Blackwill to see if she could help. While there Penny had a clear vision of a woman in a long white dress, standing beside a lake which, they assumed, was Knights Pool. Penny was sure that the woman had something important to say.

Gaynor also said that she felt the woman was trying to speak to them, to explain that there was something they must do.

Terry's wife Pat began to feel that she was being called by the woman, and on numerous occasions had the distinct impression that she was nearby. Other members of the Shotton family also felt the strange presence. Once it was so strong that it was felt in every room in the house. Terry and Pat were out at the time and only Terry's mother was home looking after the two children. She said later that 'it was as if time stood absolutely still.' She had never experienced anything like it. She had been downstairs in the living room when Terry's ten-year-old daughter came running downstairs, saying she had felt something strange in her room. The presence remained for some time before the place returned to normal.

Some days later, Pat was outside when she saw a human-sized column of what seemed to be white smoke at the bottom of the garden. At first she thought her eyes were deceiving her, but on closer examination she was certain. It was definitely there. After this she knew that the woman wished to speak through her, but was having difficulty in doing so.

A day or so later she saw the smoke again, but this time she was able to run into the house and alert Terry who also saw it.

Everyone was sure that the woman wanted to communicate with them, but the terrifying events since the finding of the Stone made them too frightened to fall into trance. Perhaps someone new would be able to go into trance to enable the woman to manifest.

Jane McKenzie, a Wolverhampton school teacher, had first met

Graham, Andy and Martin during the Autumn of 1979. Although she knew about the discovery of the Green Stone, Jane was somewhat sceptical about paranormal phenomena. That was until one night in September 1980.

That evening, as she, Graham, Martin and Jean Bosicombe, another of the teachers who shared a house with Jane, were talking in the girls' living room, Jane suddenly felt that something was happening. She lay down on the settee and fell quiet. To everyone's surprise Joanna spoke through her and announced that there was something important that they must know about the past. But the trance was not to last. Joanna apologised and said that she must go. Jane awoke and complained that she felt sick. Joanna had left since it was too risky for her to speak through Jane. Although Jane was a good subject the procedure would have apparently made her ill. She was disturbed, but not particularly frightened by the episode.

So the woman had now spoken through Jane, once again using Joanna as an intermediary. Jane felt that the woman was still nearby, and both Jean and Martin also felt her presence. She said she felt the woman could give a message to Graham, who tried to go into trance but failed to do so.

The four of them sat in the room, clearing their minds to enable the woman to communicate. Suddenly Graham saw a strange image of an Egyptian-looking building, like an ancient tomb situated in a garden. He saw two sphinxes, between which ran a corridor with a winged sun disc carved over the entrance. He knew that this building was somewhere in the Midlands, although this was preposterous. There could not possibly be such a building anywhere in England. But the image remained, and he knew that it was connected with the secret society in Victorian times. He then saw a woman, and the name *Mary Heath* came into his mind. He felt it was she who had been in charge of the secret society.

He told Terry and the others that Joanna had spoken through Jane, and what he himself had seen. But the mystery remained until Terry mentioned it to a colleague, Mike Ratcliffe, who worked in the Stoke-on-Trent Parks department. Mike, intrigued by the story, identified the building as a place in the grounds of Biddulph Grange, just to the north of Stoke-on-Trent. So the Egyptian temple actually existed.

But Graham was not the only one to experience the impression of the temple. Gaynor also saw it and said they must go there quickly.

129

She felt the woman would also be present. In addition, Marion had the impression of a path between huge pine trees leading to the temple.

Alan collected Gaynor from Oakenholt and, accompanied by Martin, Andy, Graham, Terry, Jane and Pat they visited Biddulph Grange on Sunday, 28 September.

Biddulph Grange is now an orthopaedic hospital, a fine old building rebuilt after a fire in 1897. They were intrigued to discover that on one of the remaining walls of the original building there were four circular stained glass windows depicting the mystic elements, earth, air, fire and water. Leaving the main building they made their way through a labyrinth of pathways, running between high hedges and thick shrubberies. Every so often they passed neatly-cut recesses, where, on wooden benches, patients sat talking with their visitors in the bright afternoon sunshine. After following the pathway around the flower beds and lawns, spread out before the splendid Grange, they came at last to the wide gravel trackway that Marion had described, flanked on either side by tall pines and redwoods, interspersed with the occasional stunted conifer. The path led them on, winding through the wood where the high trees cast strange shadows in the harsh sunlight. Finally it came to an end at the steps of what they first took to be a large summer house, or a lonely hermitage tucked quietly away in the secluded woodland.

When she saw the house Gaynor stopped and stared. This was it! She was sure. The pathway that her mother had seen had led them to this building. She herself recognised it, almost remembered seeing it before. When the others caught up with her they, too, stood and examined the house from a distance. Its deep red timbers against the cream coloured wall gave the quaint structure something of a bold countenance. Was this the inner sanctuary of the Order, now half overgrown by the impenetrable bushes encroaching from both sides?

Above the open doorway, supported by two carved wooden posts, was the overhanging gabled window on either side of which was painted a date in stylized figures: 1865. The year of its construction. But it was the lettering above the window that caught their attention, the letters M8M. The figure 8 with a vertical dividing line, which they recognised as a version of the ancient hermetic glyph for eternity. Could M8M symbolize the words inscribed on the sword? Meonia For(ever) Mary. If so, then it clinched the link between this place and *The Nine* in Victorian times.

When they entered the building they found themselves within a small anti-chamber, from which led two further openings. To their right was a cramped room, where in an alcove there crouched an ugly statue, seated in the cold damp interior with green fungi and mosses clinging to the walls and ceiling. It stared out along the narrow stone corridor that led away towards the light. As Gaynor examined the creature she had the impression that mystical ceremonies had once taken place there. After Andy had identified the beast as the Egyptian Ape of Thoth (2) they turned and walked through the cold passageway and emerged again into the sunshine. There could be no doubt that this was the temple Graham and Gaynor had seen in their visions. On either side of the entrance stood a large stone sphinx, facing one another, guarding the threshold of the temple. Above the entrance, in the stone-fronted facade, was a colourful depiction of the Egyptian winged sun disc. (3)

It seemed certain that this was where the secret society, *The Nine*, had met in the last century.

Gaynor found herself being drawn towards the woodland above the pathway. Something was there waiting for her, someone wanted to speak with her. As she strayed further from the path she felt it grow stronger, and she knew she was being led. Then she saw her, a young woman dressed in a flowing white dress standing beside a tree, her long brown hair bunched neatly on top of her head. The woman was looking straight at her, standing, waiting. Who was she? What did she want? Gaynor moved close enough to see that she was beautiful and of fair complexion. But as she sensed she was about to speak the woman faded and vanished before her eyes.

Upset by this episode Gaynor ran back and told Terry and then the others. When she had recovered she was able to recount that she was certain that the woman had been connected with the Temple, and that it had been 'her place'; she felt that the woman wanted desperately to tell them something.

Leaving Biddulph Grange they visited next the local parish church to make enquiries about the history of the area. There they discovered that in the last quarter of the nineteenth century Biddulph Grange was owned by Robert Heath. *Mary Heath* had been his wife. So they had been right! This mock Egyptian temple must have been the meeting place for *The Nine* in the last century, and Mary was presumably the last to lead *The Nine*. It seemed that Gaynor had experienced a vision of her at what was once her home.

So what was the message that Mary Heath was trying to impart? Before visiting Biddulph Grange Gaynor had the impression that a ceremony had once taken place somewhere in an underground chamber, and that something dreadful had happened which had caused them to flee and forced them to replace the sword with the replica they had found, years later, at Knights Pool. But how had this secret society met their end? Mary Heath was clearly trying to tell them, but she had been unable to do so.

On Sunday, 16 November, 1980, at one thirty, Penny Blackwill had a vision of a large house and a bearded man, who, by his clothes, must have lived there during the Victorian era. She knew there was something very wrong about this man and that she must immediately tell Terry. As she sketched her impression she saw him again, but now he stood next to a fire. She felt that he meant 'danger for all', and wrote these words beside her drawing of the man. She then sensed that he meant to destroy someone, and she began to write down the impressions as they flooded in, accompanied by further sketches. She knew this was of great importance to them all.

The scene then changed and she saw robed figures which at first she thought were monks. Then followed a woman dressed in 'old-fashioned clothes', whom she recognised as the same person she had seen standing beside the lake. In the distance a dog was barking, and there were people standing in a circle with one in the centre. She knew they were in an underground chamber somewhere, with gold-coloured plates and other artefacts placed round the circle. A sudden horror overcame her. She saw that they were making the wrong moves, and that there was a great danger of their being destroyed.

Penny quickly wrote it all down, then dated and signed it to give to Terry. She had no idea what it meant, but it was imperative that he should have it. Her insistence that this was vital prompted him to see Graham on Tuesday 18 November.

That evening Terry, Graham and Jane sat in Jane's house discussing the recent events and the meaning of Penny's visions. They decided that the woman trying to pass the message to them was Mary Heath, who was showing her what had become of her secret society, and that the tall, dark-bearded man had somehow done great harm to them at the time. Had she seen Mary Heath preparing a ceremony, somewhere in an underground chamber, and the man trying to destroy them? Their ceremony had failed. Had this failure resulted as Gaynor had felt in the untimely end of the *The Nine* and of Mary Heath's society?

They must discover what had happened to Mary Heath and her Order. This was the crux of the whole affair. Penny had said that Terry, Alan and the others, without precautions, would meet the same fate. They had to know. But how were they to find out? How could they communicate with Mary Heath?

Around nine thirty p.m. Terry made a suggestion. Perhaps they could attempt some form of *séance*. He did not like the idea, but it was the only way left to discover the answers they needed. They were not experts in communicating with spirits, but there was no choice. Something was trying to get through and was experiencing difficulties because of their fears about falling into trance. If they made a makeshift ouija board it would perhaps unconciously guide their fingers and they would be safe in not knowing who was being controlled. Whether spirits exist in the sense that some people believe, they did not know, but they were aware that usually the glass is moved unconsciously by the participants.

They made up letters of the alphabet and found a glass. After some minutes of apprehension and garbled nonsense, the latter began to move more purposefully round the table. They asked if someone was there and it spelt YES. Next they asked if they had managed to tune in to the source of the psychic messages and again it spelt YES.

Was Penny's message important? The glass repeatedly spelt YES until they instructed it to stop. Then they asked more questions:

Q. Do you have something to tell us?

A. *Yes*

Q. Has it to do with this underground place that Penny and Gaynor saw?

A. *Yes*

Q. Where is it?

A. *Wolverhampton*

Terry then felt that the underground chamber was near the old house where Penny said the bearded man had lived. The glass confirmed this.

Q. Was his house in Wolverhampton too?

A. *Yes*

Q. Whereabouts?

A. *It was a school*
Q. What is the name of the school?
A. *The Catherine Geney School*.
Q. Is it a school now?
A. *No*

To their amazement the glass spelt out that the school once stood in Oaks Crescent. This was surely too incredible to be true but could be checked.

Q. Was the underground place that Penny saw below the school?
A. *Nearby*.

Then they asked if it was correct that the ceremony took place in a cellar in, or near, Oaks Crescent, and if it involved Mary Heath. It answered YES. But could this be correct? The glass repeated that it was so.

Q. When was this ceremony?
A. *The 22nd of November, 1875*.

They then asked where exactly the cellar was, but the answer was unclear. However, it did say that something terrible had happened there which brought about the end of the Order. They must, it said, now put this wrong to right in order to release the power of the Stone. They must go to the place and banish the evil guardian that held this power.

The underground chamber was a cellar below a house, and a tunnel led from it to another chamber where the power was held. To this they must go. It then surprised them all by saying that it referred to the old cellars below the Oaks Crescent flat! This was too ridiculous for words.

They asked if the cellars in Penny and Gaynor's vision were indeed the cellars below Graham's flat, but it would not answer. It repeated that this *chamber* was there in 1875, once again spelling out that this was where the power was now held. It was no coincidence that the flat was their headquarters.

'But I chose that place,' Graham objected.

'*Can you remember how you found it?*' the glass answered.

'Yes. A girl I knew whose brother lived there was moving out and she told me about it.'

'*Your meeting with her was no coincidence,*' it answered.

Graham removed his finger and sat back. This was too much! Terry then asked if it had all begun to happen because they had taken the

Oaks Crescent flat. Yes, it answered. They had been chosen and the circumstances had been created to permit them to move into the flat. Graham objected, saying this was going too far. He refused to continue.

Jane —   Q. Was this power held because of the ceremony going wrong?

          A. *Yes.*

Terry —   Q. Was it to do with the bearded man who Penny thought destroyed them?

          A. *Yes.*

          Q. Who was he?

          A. *John Laing.* (4)

          Q. Who is John Laing?

It answered that Laing was a black magician through whom all the power of the Evil One was wielded in 1875.

Terry —   Q. How did he manage to destroy them?

          A. *They made incorrect moves.*

          Q. In what way?

It did not answer.

          Q. Who are you?

Still it would not answer. Instead it told them that it would explain how they must banish the evil to release the power from the cellar.

Jane —   Q. How do we know it's not a trick? You may be Laing.

The glass did not move.

Graham —Are you Mary Heath?

          A. *Yes*

          Q. Were you the last leader of The Nine?

          A. *Yes*

          Q. How do we know you are Mary Heath and not something or someone evil.

          A. *I will tell Marion. She knows what you have to do.*

They agreed that if she accomplished this then it must be Mary Heath, reasoning that nothing evil could penetrate Marion's mind. They phoned Marion but told her nothing of the *séance*. She said that just before they phoned she had the vivid image of an eight-pointed star enter her mind. Then an underground passageway bricked up with rubble. Following this she gave an exact description of the cellars below the Oaks Crescent flat. 'You must go there and draw the star' she said. 'You have to do something, but I'm not sure what'.

As Marion knew nothing of Penny's vision or their *séance*, they were shocked. Most of all because she had described the cellars which she had never actually seen.

They told her they would explain later and returned to the board.

Terry —   Q. Is Marion right?

A. *Yes, it is the eight-pointed star of Michael.*

Q. What does this mean?

A. *Use the symbol.*

Q. Are we to banish this evil with it?

A. *Yes.*

Q. How do we do that?

A. *By calling upon the force of St. Michael.*

Q. How?

It did not answer.

Q. What happened in 1875, on 22 November?

A. *On that day the Evil One, working through Laing, launched a great force against us and our power was destroyed.*

Q. How could he do that?

A. *We did not use the Stone.*

Q. But you knew where it was.

A. *Yes. But we did not dare use it. Too many of us had already been corrupted by the power we held. We had to ward off his attack, if we could, without it. If we gathered the full force of the Stone we might have, in our weakness, lost it to him.*

Q. But he beat you?

A. *Yes. He destroyed the Order of Meonia.*

Q. Is that what you were called?

A. *Yes.*

Q. Did you all die?

A. *Not immediately.*

Q. But shortly after at the fishing village?

A. *Some of us.*

Q. What happened then?

A. *We knew that the Order would be rekindled to continue the work and complete our task.*

Q. Is that us?

A. *Yes.*

Q. And you brought us together?

A. *Yes.*

Q. How?

It did not answer.

A. *You must repossess the power that will enable you to complete the Stone.*

Q. How?

A. *Marion will tell you.*

At that moment the phone rang. It was Marion. She had just had a vision of a cellar with a huge eight-pointed star painted on the floor and a mystical ceremony in progress. She said that this had happened many years ago, and when it had gone wrong some powerful influence had remained behind in the place to contain a great force the defeated Order had possessed. They could now release it by calling upon St. Michael and performing a banishment.

The glass moved no more. It was 1.00 a.m. 19 November, 1980.

20 November

In the old town records at the Wolverhampton reference library they checked the facts. The Catherine Geney School was indeed in Oaks Crescent during 1875, and the mysterious Mr. Laing had been a real person associated with the school.

That evening Terry and Alan visited Jane and were joined by Graham and a little later by Mike Ratcliffe, who had become interested in the story because of its links with Biddulph Grange. Before leaving Terry's, Alan had a strong impression that he should take some holy water. Terry's wife Pat, being a Catholic, had a phial of water from the grotto at Lourdes, given to her by a close friend. Alan felt this would suffice and, generously, she let him have it.

That evening they again used the glass and letters and, as previously, it spelt out the information. It explained that by the 1870's the Order of Meonia had discovered that the Evil One had been using John Laing and his black magic group in much the same way as it had used the dark-haired woman and the Warwickshire witch coven.

John Laing had lived in Wolverhampton, so a member of the Order of Meonia, a chemist, Thomas Reade, took a house in Oaks Crescent so that they could observe his activities. By November 1875 Laing had used his power to corrupt the Order and had caused them considerable trouble. However, Mary Heath, the leader, refused to use the Stone because she felt that they were insufficiently powerful to repel the force of the Evil One. If they tried and failed they might then risk the destruction of the Stone. They decided instead to try to break the influence of Laing on 22 November 1875 by their mystical knowledge. Their efforts failed and the occult battle was lost, and with it much of their power. Their protection now gone, the group fled, some falling ill, and others even dying a short while later.

Throughout the years all the leaders of the Order inherited a mystical amulet, a key to unlock the full potential of the Meonia Stone. It had been a small silver cross containing a mysterious power. When the malefic being itself manifested in the cellar, its force was so great that the power of the silver cross was erased. Although the cross itself had been destroyed, the influence it had contained was still held in the atmosphere of the cellar. Knowing all was lost and that they no longer possessed the power to release it, Mary Heath disbanded the Order. She would utilise her remaining power and knowledge to one day bring the Order together again. This was what was now happening. She had drawn them together to complete her work, those who were psychic, and some who were merely investigators.

But why had she disbanded the Order? The answer was clear.

It spelt out: '*The seeds of destruction lie within, as you were told. This has resulted in the failure of The Nine so many times in the past, and why they have never destroyed the evil being we sought to oppose*'. Many of their Order had been corrupted by the power and their secret knowledge. Thus their successive leaders had elected to leave the Stone hidden. '*There is a fine line between power used for preservation and power used for gain*', the glass spelt out. Mary Heath deemed that the only way to recover their power from the 'Evil One' was to begin anew, and for those who inherited the task to be unaware of how to wield their inheritance for personal gain. Thus, *they* had been chosen.

But why had she not used the Stone to reflect its attack in 1875?

In their weakened state the risk of losing the Stone was too great; their own corruption and hatred had weakened the strength to use it correctly. The force of the Evil One could therefore have destroyed the Stone. After their failure in the cellar the infernal guardian now held the key to the ultimate power of the Stone, thus preventing it from being used.

Q. But does the Stone not already have power?

A. *Yes. But the only power remaining in it is the power necessary to reflect his attacks. If used correctly the full power of the Stone can destroy him.*

They then asked if 'he' could 'tune in' to this communication? It answered no, not since Gaynor had repelled his attack.

They had many other questions. What had happened to Pakington's original sword? How were UFOs involved? How had it all begun? And, most importantly, where was it all leading? The spirit refused to answer. There was something they must do now; release the key to the power of the Stone. The spirit told them that it would take too long to explain by using the glass. Instead it would inform Marion Sunderland. Seconds afterwards the phone rang. It was Marion.

She had just had a powerful vision. They must go immediately to the cellar, draw an eight-pointed star on a piece of card, stand in a circle and call upon the force of St. Michael.

The force to hold the key had been cast by Satanism; therefore they must use an old banishment to break it. Since they had not been corrupted they could succeed where Mary Heath and the Order of Meonia had failed. She asked them to get a pen and paper and write down what she told them.

They must go, she said, to the cellar and sprinkle a circle of holy water around them. Graham told her this was impossible. How were they to obtain holy water? But Marion had the impression that they had some and that he should check. He asked the others and Alan produced the phial of Lourdes water he had felt impelled to bring. No-one but Terry knew of this, and certainly not Marion. She then instructed them to take a rosary blessed by a priest. Again Graham protested, but she assured him she was being told that they did have one. He checked. Alan, Terry and Jane shook their heads. Mike looked astonished and produced a rosary, adding that it had been blessed.

Graham returned to the phone. Marion said: 'Somebody must hold the rosary high above his head and perform the act of banishment.' As he scribbled down the instructions, Marion explained that they must draw an eight-pointed star and lay it between them as they reached the cellar. As the star of St. Michael, it would act as a point of concentration. When Graham asked her to describe exactly what the star looked like Marion thought for a moment.

'I've just been advised that one of you has been told to draw it.'

Graham hurried to the others. To his astonishment he saw that Terry had at that instant received a psychic impression to construct the eight-pointed star which he was now drawing. There was no doubt that the simultaneous impressions proved that they were meant to perform the banishment.

The final thing they needed was salt, said Marion, to cast a circle of protection round them. Her impressions continued, and she next received a string of words. Graham was told to write them down exactly as she gave them. They must recite the words in the cellar, and, following this invocation, banish the guardian with more words to invoke the symbolic power of the Archangel Michael.

Now they must go and perform the banishment.

At ten o'clock the five made their way to the Oaks Crescent flat. They pulled aside the trap-door beneath the hall carpet, and by candlelight descended into the dark cellar. A narrow passage leads to the main room, a cold, stone chamber of whitewashed brick about five yards square. The flickering candles cast long shadows on the peeling whitewash as they formed a circle. Alan had remained outside, waiting to run for help if things went wrong.

Graham sprinkled the salt and holy water round them as Mike held the crucifix. Terry then read aloud the words Marion had given them to summon the Archangel Michael.

'Archangel Michael. I adjure thee in the name of the blessed Virgin, by her holy body, by her sanctified body, by her sanctified soul, to come forth. I ask thee by all the holy names, bring thy legions of angels.'

These words were followed by other words she had given to banish the guardian.

As Terry finished they all felt a tremendous surge of power flood through them. Everywhere was calm and still in the hitherto disturbed atmosphere of the cold cellar.

Leaving, they returned to Jane's house and phoned Marion, who was certain they had succeeded in banishing the guardian and releasing the key to unlock the power of the Stone.

The following day Graham and Jane checked many of the facts in the Wolverhampton records. They discovered that Thomas Reade had indeed existed and had lived at Number 2, Oaks Crescent in 1875. They were unable to establish exactly where Number 2 had been, since all the houses were now different. But Number 2 appeared to have been at least near the site upon which 19 Oaks Crescent now stood. The building plans for the present house no longer exist. Whether the cellars were there in the Victorian period, or a tunnel had led there, or if they were one and the same, remained unknown.

Now, with the banishment successfully accomplished, how were they to gain the full power of the Stone?

Later that night Jane was at home when she suddenly experienced the strange feeling that a message was being given to her. She saw a woman in white standing beside an old stone cross. This vision, she knew, had something to do with their reinheriting the power of the Stone.

That night Alan went to the Sunderlands', and there he, Marion and Fred used the glass and letters in an attempt to obtain further information. It said simply that the evil had been banished from the cellar in Oaks Crescent, and they could now find the power of the Stone.

That something powerful had taken place was confirmed when Andy, now living in Essex, came to stay the weekend in Wolverhampton on Friday, 21 November. That evening Andy and Graham decided to take a look at the empty cellar. Perhaps there would be some indication that the tunnel once led into it, or that the cellar itself had been there in the Victorian period.

As they examined the brickwork in the main chamber they heard a deep groaning noise. They froze. They then heard the noise of someone or something clambering down the pile of magazines in the corridor and into the cellar. They stood petrified as the noise grew louder, approaching quickly and now only just round the corner. As they waited in the near darkness they had no idea what might emerge from the passageway. Silence. There was not a sound in the cold cellar. The seconds seemed like hours as they edged forward nervously, glancing into the passage. There was nothing there. Quickly they scrambled up the piles of magazines and out of the cellar.

Had they, they wondered, heard the last fading energies of the evil guardian that for so long had held the key to unlock the power of the Stone?

That night something remarkable took place. Gaynor suddenly awoke to find herself in a wide open void, a white marble floor stretching to infinity around her. A figure, the woman she had seen at Biddulph Grange in a white flowing gown, approached and gave her a silver cross. She said the cross now held a power to call upon a guardian. The woman explained, but Gaynor could not understand, except that it would act something like a radio.

Gaynor awoke to find the silver cross still in her hand! She recognised it as her own cross. Everyone was astonished. She had lost it months before in the town. The woman, presumably Mary Heath, had returned it by supernatural means they could not even begin to understand.

It appeared that the key to summon the power of the Stone that they had released from the cellar and was once focussed in Mary Heath's pendant, had now been restored in Gaynor's cross.

At last they had the key to unlock the power of the Meonia Stone.

Chapter Fourteen

---•---

The Reawakening

CHRISTMAS 1980. Marion and Fred had invited Graham to spend Christmas with them at their home in North Wales. It would be an ideal opportunity to relax and reflect on the events to date. However, many questions were still unanswered. What was the ultimate purpose of the Meonia Stone? What were they to do where Mary Heath and the Order of Meonia had failed?

Boxing Day 1980 was to bring new answers. That night Graham experienced a vivid dream, in which he saw what he took to be the Pharoah Akhenaten lying on a stone slab in an underground chamber adorned with hieroglyphics. In his headband was a small green stone — the Meonia Stone. Around the slab stood a number of small white pyramids. A procession filed into the chamber, each picking up a pyramid and making their way from the tomb along a stone corridor.

As he dreamt he had the impression that the centre of learning — Akhet-aten had fallen to their adversaries, the followers of the Amon religion.(1) Akhenaten's people knew this, and were preparing to leave for Britain with the Stone and these nine small pyramids. What they were Graham did not know, but as he awoke the words, *the nine lights* were still clear in his mind.

He was immensely puzzled. Why should he have dreamt this? What could it mean? Perhaps Gaynor would know. In the automatic writings that followed they found their answer.

The pyramids each contained an aspect of power, one of nine aspects necessary to use the Meonia Stone. When Akhenaten died, his Egyptian followers knew that their task had failed, and that their

143

centre of learning would soon fall. The power of the Stone, being so potentially destructive, was taken from it and split into nine separate parts. Each of these nine pyramids contained one aspect of the power of the Stone.

The party came to Britain to establish a secret Order and preserve some of the knowledge of the Megalithic culture with which to resist the workings of the Evil One. The Stone could be used to ward off this force, but its full power was divided into the *Nine Lights* to prevent its misuse.

If the energy of the Stone was complete, and it was misused, it could result in the end of the Stone, which was the only means of finally destroying the Evil One.

Before establishing their colony in the centre of England, the Egyptians first travelled to Southern England. There, at nine sites sacred to the Megalithic culture, they transferred the power of the Nine Lights from the pyramids into the sites. Nine aspects of power necessary to realise the full potential of the Meonia Stone.

So the next part of their quest was to relocate these Lights and to channel them back into the Stone. Since Akhenaten this had not been achieved. His Egyptian followers had brought and left these powers so that when the time was right they could be repossessed by those who held the Stone.

They must begin their search on New Year's Day 1981, the search for the first four of the Nine Lights.

Gaynor asked who she was communicating with, and was told that it was the *spirit guide* to the First Light. Ideally it was she who should carry out the search, but she was too young and vulnerable to risk so dangerous a quest. Others must be chosen. But who could she choose? Not her mother, for she had to look after her younger brothers and sisters. Terry, Martin and Alan? Of course. But no, they had to work and she knew the search might take weeks. That something so important and unusual should be stopped by something so normal was a paradox. She was left with only one choice: Graham, who must also take Andy. Perhaps Terry and Alan could help along the way? She knew that whoever went would immediately become psychically attuned to the guides, since they possessed the Stone.

Graham was concerned. How could he accept something so important? Suppose he failed? And how was he to obtain the information?

Gaynor knew. He must take the pencil as she had done and put it to paper. The guide to the First Light would write through him and communicate that way. Half-heartedly he agreed. If Gaynor said so then he had to try it.

He took the pencil. Who or what were they communicating with? It confirmed that it was the *guide* to the First Light, and went on to explain that they were now seeking the first four. Each one would be at a site important to the Megalithic culture, and at each site there would be a *spirit guide* to the Light. There would also be a *spirit guardian*, and finally a living person who would guide them to this guardian.

This was the process to find each Light. They had first to be led to the site by the *spirit guide*. Then they must find the person who would tell them of a local tradition or legend about the mythical or symbolic *spirit guardian*. They must then summon this *spirit guardian* and the energy would be transferred back into the Stone. Throughout history the leader of the Order was given the key to release the *guide* to the first Light. At any time the Order could have regained the Lights, but because of the risks involved in fully charging the Stone they had never done so.

But how could people today lead them to an energy stored over 3,000 years ago? The *guide* gave its answer. The Stone and the Lights had been programmed to ensure this. When the *guide* to the First Light was released, this programming became immediately effective. Whatever circumstances were necessary to find the Lights would be established and set in motion by the Lights themselves. This process was too complex to explain; they must simply accept that it would happen. The banishment performed on 18 November, 1980 had enabled Gaynor's White Lady to release the *guide* to the First Light.

They must now find the first four. Then would follow the second four and finally, the ninth Light that would link them as one.

The *guide* said that the First Light was near Dorchester, in Oxfordshire. But how would they know where to begin? The parting words were that they would soon know.

Graham was flabbergasted. This was simply not possible. But again, as so many times before, he reflected on the recent past. Everything else had been impossible so why should this be different? Besides, perhaps it was not so ridiculous. As an investigator he knew that many of the things that had occurred were not as impossible as they might have appeared since most paranormal experiences occur using the available belief systems of the person who witnesses them. Seen in this way it was perhaps not so unbelievable.

★ ★ ★ ★

Barry Sunderland was psychic. He claimed to have had psychic experiences but he had never done automatic writing or drawing like Gaynor and Andrew James. As he handed his mother his drawing of the old stone cross he knew it was important. Something had told him to draw it and that Gaynor and Graham must have it.

★ ★ ★ ★

Barry's drawing came only seconds after the end of the communication. An old cross and Dorchester? Not much to act on, but what was there to lose? A trip to Dorchester could do no harm. And if it was correct Graham couldn't let the others down. He telephoned Andy and told him the details. They would *rendezvous* in Dorchester on New Year's Day.

On New Year's Eve Graham, Terry and Mike stood in a field near Terry's house in Saverley Green. He explained how the night before he had tried to concentrate his thoughts in order to obtain information about the First Light. A vivid image flashed into his mind's eye: a carved figure of a man sleeping, with a strange diagram like the Hebrew tree of life in the stained-glass window above him. Terry knew it was connected with the First Light, and when they found this they would be on the right track.

Gaynor had suggested they stand in the field and attempt again to communicate with the *guide*. As Graham held the Stone he heard the words, *'Follow the Neots until you reach the Waters of Isis. There you will find the one who will tell you of the guardian at the place of the First Light.'* In his mind he saw the image of two long earth banks.

★ ★ ★ ★

New Year's Day. Graham, Terry and Mike met Andy and Peter Marlow in Dorchester. Peter was a London businessman who had generously offered to finance the search for the Lights.

At last they found it, a tall stone cross outside Dorchester Abbey, which was itself interesting since it was a Rose Cross as Barry had drawn, and dated back to medieval times.

Inside the Abbey Terry stared at the stone carving of the sleeping man, and above him the brightly coloured stained-glass window depicting the Tree of Life.

'Amazing!' he said. 'It's exactly as I saw it.'

They stared in disbelief at the huge banks of earth stretching before them into the far distance. This ancient earthwork, presumably the 'Neots', stands twenty to thirty feet high and stretches for about half a mile. Divided by a ditch, the two grass-covered banks, about ten yards wide, run almost parallel, and are about thirty yards apart. They later discovered that the banks form part of the Dyke Hills, a promontory fort which dates from the Iron Age.

'Follow the Neots,' had been their instruction. The afternoon sun made it fresh and warm as they walked in single file along the well-trodden pathway on top of the earth banks.

After half a mile they reached a wide river ahead. They had followed the Neots, but there was no sign of anyone. Here the river split into two, and a small foot-bridge led to a hut on the island dividing the two water courses. It housed the only person for miles around, the keeper of the lock.

Andy suggested that the only person who could possibly be the one they were looking for was the lock keeper. They would have to ask him. Could he tell them of the mythical *spirit guardian* whom they would then have to summon?

They told him that they were researching traditions and legends in the area. But he knew of no such legend. Andy asked him about the river. Did he know of anything called the Waters of Isis? It was the Thames, he replied, and that particular stretch of water was, in fact, called the Isis. They were taken aback. Everything else was correct, but where was the person who would know?

As they were about to leave, the lock keeper said he had just remembered something. There *was* a local legend. It was rather odd that they should have mentioned it, for only a short time ago he had been reading an old book and had come across a legend associated with a nearby hill-fort. He pointed to a high hill across the river, and said that legend spoke of buried treasure there, protected by a guardian spirit that assumed the form of a raven.

They were astonished, for they had been on the point of leaving just

147

when he had recalled it. Was it coincidence? They would have to wait until tomorrow to find out. It was now around four o'clock and growing dark. That night Alan, Mike and Peter returned home in order to resume work after the holiday.

The following day when Andy and Graham returned, the lock keeper showed them the notes he had made, then directed them to the hill-fort. They thanked him and hurried from his small hut. It was around ten o'clock, and the January morning was cold and crisp. The hill was a mile or so distant, as they walked back to the car.

They parked and made their way to the old hill-fort, walking up the steep hill and passing through an old wooden gate. Later, they discovered that it was called Castle Hill and dates back to the Iron Age.

The fort was impressive, a large, roughly circular ditch about a hundred yards in diameter. The ditch was wide and deep, and as they walked around it they decided that even if it had not been in existence in Megalithic times, it could well have been constructed on an earlier Megalithic site. On the central plateau grew a small wood. Crows nests stood out high in the trees, the birds occasionally alighting onto the thin branches.

As they walked along the dry ditch they discussed what to do. Presumably they should summon the *guardian*. Graham was apprehensive. Summoning raven guardians was not to his liking. Neither was it to Andy's, but they knew it was not real. At least not in the sense of actually summoning a celestial raven. They must go through the motions of releasing the power from the site back into the Stone. They had to follow this belief system, otherwise they would never know if the Lights truly existed.

Who would do it? Graham asked Andy, who felt it best to take Gaynor's advice. She had chosen Graham, and Andy was to accompany him. He had no choice.

As they walked into the middle of the wood he took the Stone in his right hand. Only a light breeze brushed through the trees that winter morning as they stood alone on the ancient fort. Andy backed away, uncertain what to expect. What would Graham do? Graham himself had no idea.

'Just say the first thing that comes into your head,' said Andy.

Graham laughed, shook his head and spoke, his arms stretched out as he held the Stone.

148

'Raven Guardian, whoever or whatever you are, give us the First Light.'

For a moment there was nothing. Then he felt it. A tingling sensation in his right hand in which he held the Stone. As he felt it the wind blew harder. Andy looked towards the trees in front of Graham. The tingling grew, flowing through his arm and into his body, gushing into his entire being. A warmth, an exhilarating, almost sensual, glow of energy, passing through every vein and nerve ending.

Suddenly the wind whipped up, racing from tree to tree towards them. Andy stared. He could not believe it. In seconds it swirled across the plateau, howling around the fort, an angry blast gushing over them. The two solitary figures were nearly bowled over. Graham almost fell to the ground. Andy raced to the nearest tree and grabbed hold of it, looking back towards Graham. As the wind howled to a crescendo the dark birds flew from their nests and circled above them, shrieking and crying as they were blown about the sky on the violent eddies of air.

As suddenly as the gale came it had gone. The glow flooded from him and back into the Stone. Graham opened his eyes.

'Bloody hell!' He clasped the Stone tightly in his hand. 'We've got it, but I don't know how.' He felt uplifted. All he knew was that the Stone had absorbed the first Light.

'I don't believe it,' said Andy. 'The wind, the birds. It was incredible. Impossible.'

They could not deny it. It had happened. They had both seen the wind grow from a light breeze to a raging gale, the crows circling around them as Graham felt the fearsome sensation. They had the First Light.

But he still had to know from Gaynor. Quickly they left the fort and made their way to a call box.

Gaynor knew. The First Light was safe, back in the Stone where it truly belonged. Yes, they had it, she was certain. Now they must go on to the Uffington White Horse. It was somewhere near there that they would find the Second Light.

High on the Berkshire Downs is the White Horse of Uffington, a huge chalk figure carved by a Celtic tribe before the Roman invasion.

The carving is 374 feet long, and archaeologists have dated it from at least 100 B.C. On top of the hill stands Uffington Castle, an Iron Age hill-fort consisting of a shallow ditch with earth banks covering about eight acres.

They parked their car and walked to the top of the hill. The mid-afternoon was cold as they stood on the fort, surveying the vast expanse of flat terrain before them.

Wondering what their next move should be Andy suggested that Graham should again hold the Stone. As he did so he turned and looked towards a small copse of trees on the distant horizon. Somehow he knew their answer lay there. A narrow track led from the fort to the wood, forming part of the Ridgeway, a prehistoric trade route that runs across Southern England from Dover to Ilchester. As they followed it darkness began to close in.

Wayland's Smithy. The stones of the long-chambered barrow stood tall and proud as they approached. Surrounded by a copse of trees the low earth mound is about fifty yards long and ten yards wide, an ancient barrow over 5,000 years old. One end is higher and here stand the erect standing stones, the gateway to a small chamber within. Graham had no idea that the chamber was inside the copse, and Andy had only heard of Wayland's Smithy during his studies of Megalithic sites. The barrow derives its name from Wieland the Smith, the blacksmith of the Gods in German and Scandinavian mythology.

As dusk fell the two men crouched uncomfortably in the low chamber inside the barrow, talking for a short while, but as darkness came they had still not resolved what course to take next. Andy suggested that Graham should hold the Stone and summon the second *guardian*, although they had no idea the form it would adopt. As he did so a distant rumbling echoed through the chamber. Within seconds it grew louder and the ground began to shake about them. It gathered resonance and volume, as if hundreds of horses were in stampede across the barrow above them, building up to an almost deafening crescendo.

Abruptly it was gone. All was still in the chamber as they exchanged glances. A moment of silence; then, as if from all around the barrow, came the strangest sound. A distinct tinkling, like the sound of wind chimes played at random drifting in on the air. The noise was too clear and discernable to be the wind whistling through the trees. It grew louder, the high tones resonating musically around them. Then, suddenly, it too had ceased. They held their breath and waited.

'Have you got the Light?' Andy asked, after a few long seconds.

Graham shook his head, 'No, nothing happened at all.'

They scrambled out of the chamber into the darkness. No-one in sight, nothing to account for the eerie noises they had heard. They had not released the Second Light, but by using the Stone they had certainly done something. They would never know the nature of the mythical *spirit guardian* until they had found the person they should look for.

They walked along the pathway back to the car. As darkness fell it seemed they were hardly nearer to finding the Second Light.

Back at the hotel they reasoned that, as in the case of the First Light, the person who knew of the *guardian* might well be someone working or living nearby, perhaps a forestry commissioner or the person responsible for the land the chamber was on. They decided to return next morning and carry out the search.

As they were parking their car near the barrow at about 9.00 a.m. a white Range Rover pulled up beside them. They decided to ask the owner and his young son, who had also alighted to visit the Smithy, if they knew of any local legends associated with the place. To their surprise he was the local forest warden; however, he was a newcomer to the district and couldn't help them. It was his son who suddenly looked up and said that there was a story associated with the ancient barrow. In legend, treasure was supposed to be buried beneath the chamber, and to find it you must kneel on the top, bow three times and ask for help from the elves who guarded it.

Andy and Graham were astonished. They did not believe in elves, but they had to do it, go through the motions, as they had with the raven, of summoning this mythical guardian. In a way they couldn't understand, this process acted as a release system for the Light to transfer it from the site and back into the Stone.

Graham knelt on the chamber, with the Stone in his hand, bowed three times and asked for help. As he summoned the *guardians*, the light breeze changed to a howling gale. The trees in the copse blew wildly as he again felt the energy surging from the Stone, powering through his body and subsiding as the howling wind dropped to the former breeze.

They had the Second Light.

151

The Third Light was at the Avebury stone circle near the Marlborough Downs. There, the village of Avebury is scattered in and around the enormous circle of sarsen stones which have been dated to 2,000 B.C. Many of them were destroyed in the seventeenth and eighteenth centuries, and used to build Avebury village and the nearby farms. The circular bank of grass-covered chalk is 1,400 feet in diameter and has an inner ditch some thirty feet deep, giving a depth from the bottom of the ditch to the top of the bank of fifty five feet. The circle is huge and impressive, a timeless monument to the achievements of the Megalithic culture.

In 1724, Dr. William Stukeley, a noted antiquarian, made an engraving of the site as it then looked. He saw that it represented the solar serpent, formed by the circle and two avenues of stones stretching for more than a mile each to the south-east and south-west. The south-east avenue ends in a stone circle 130 feet in diameter, called the Sanctuary, on top of Overton Hill. Sadly, the second avenue no longer exists. Stukely considered that the site represented the solar serpent of the ancient Egyptians, a symbol representing the highest ideals of inner truths and the supreme creative being. They could see why the Egyptians had chosen the monument as a location to hold the Third Light.

En route to the circle Graham held the Stone and had the vague impression that a stampede of horses was involved with the summoning of this particular Light.

As they parked their car in the village Andy mentioned that years earlier he had visited the circle with John and Sue Avis, the UFO abductees, to research into their psychic abilities at the site. At lunchtime they had been in a pub having a drink, discussing the day ahead, when John suddenly had the unexpected psychic impression that here there was someone who would one day guide them to something, and that she was a woman who worked behind the bar at that very inn! At the time they could not explain John's strange impression, and dismissed it from their minds. Now, years later, the meaning became clear. Before calling in at the pub they had asked a local shop proprietor if he knew of any legends about a stampede of horses. He did not, but said there was a woman who would know, who at one time claimed to have had a strange experience involving phantom horses. She was a local and her name was Heather Garland. If she was not at home they would be able to find her that evening at the village inn where she worked. By now they were hardly surprised to find that the pub was the same which Andy and John had visited all those years before.

On calling they found no-one home. But as they left the cottage they saw a woman walking across the circle. Andy suddenly felt that this was Heather. He was right.

She told them she used to ride her horse along the nearby Ridgeway. One night she had heard a ghostly stampede of horses which approached and passed straight through her.

This must be it.

They made their way to the section of the Ridgeway where Heather had experienced the stampede, and as they stood between two old stones Graham held the Meonia Stone. Again the light breeze suddenly rose to a howling wind. Then he knew that the Third Light would be found between two large standing stones in the village.

Standing between the two grey stones, known locally as The Cove, Graham clasped the Stone and summoned the *spirit guardian*. For the third time he felt the same glowing sensation from the Stone rising through his body and subsiding back along his arm as the Third Light entered the small green gem clasped firmly in his hand.

After hundreds of years of lying dormant in the fields of Avebury, the Third Light of power was once again returned to the Meonia Stone.

Once more they telephoned Marion to ask Gaynor for confirmation that all was well. It was, she said, and they must continue.

The Fourth Light was at Glastonbury Tor.

That night, back in the hotel, Graham held the Stone and felt that it was important for Alan and Terry to help with the search. They telephoned them and arranged a *rendezvous* the following day outside Glastonbury Abbey.

When they met, they discovered the reason for Alan being there. The previous night he had had a vivid dream of a house at the foot of Glastonbury Tor, where he was sure they would find the person who would know of the mythical *spirit guardian*.

That afternoon the four of them made their way from the Abbey to the ancient Tor of Glastonbury. The 500-foot hill towers above the

153

surrounding plane, a site of so many ancient legends and scenic beauty that every year thousands of tourists climb to the summit to gaze over the Somerset plain below.

All that remains of the church on the Tor, erected to the memory of St. Michael, is a rectangular stone tower, the adjoining church having been wrecked by an earth tremor some hundreds of years ago. Archaeologists claim that a group of hermits founded Britain's first monastery on the site as long ago as the fourth century. It is believed there was also a Megalithic stone circle on the Tor, long since destroyed, some of the stones behing used to build Glastonbury Abbey. (2).

As they drove along the road at the base of the Tor, searching for the house that Alan had dreamt of, a small dwelling marked St. Michael's Cottage caught Terry's eye. He had a feeling that this was where the person lived.

To their surprise, the young girl who answered the door told Andy of the legendary associations of a phoenix with the Tor. Again they had it, the *spirit guardian*, a phoenix, the fire-bird that perishes in its own flames to be reborn anew.

They made their way to the summit, arriving as the sun slipped below the horizon. On the tower was the carving of a phoenix, and, as Graham again held the Stone, the now familiar surge of power once more flooded through him. Terry and Alan stepped back in shock as the wind howled for a fourth time, almost bowling them from the Tor. A number of tourists standing round looked about them in confusion as the wind abruptly ceased.

The Fourth Light had been returned to the Meonia Stone.

The quest for the first four Lights was now complete. How or what had happened was beyond them, but all were witness to the remarkable events accompanying the return of the first four aspects of power to the Stone.

A few days later Alan, Terry and Mike took the Stone to Penny Blackwill in Staffordshire. She took it in her hand. As she did she felt that it now possessed a greater power than when she had last held it. As they passed it round they saw it change to a deeper shade of green and felt it grow hotter and heavier as each held it.

So ended the first quest for the Lights. Some weeks were to pass before they would again be called to search. Until then Gaynor decided that they must wait and be patient.

Chapter Fifteen

The White Dragon

IT was dark. The tall shadowy figure was less than a hundred yards away, walking slowly to the top of the road. He was dressed entirely in black, with a long coat reaching well below his knees and on his head a wide-brimmed hat. A black dog pattered obediently beside him.

As she followed him that night she instinctively felt there was something wrong. She had known that feeling before, the sense that something was not as it should be. To the left of the footpath were open fields, to her right the familiar row of houses past which she usually walked the dog.

The man looked back. She could see him clearly in the light of the streetlamps. What was it about him? Was he not simply a local walking his dog? It was his walk, the coat, the hat. Surely no-one still wore such wide-brimmed hats?

She moved more quickly, hoping to draw nearer for a closer look. The man continued walking. She moved faster; it would take only a few seconds to get significantly nearer. So why was he still so far away? Each time she increased her steps she gained no ground. However quickly she moved he remained the same distance away.

Pirehill Lane ceases to be a minor road and becomes a track, rising gently onto the hill after which it is named. Here the houses end and a small stream crosses at right angles beneath the road. Opposite the last house are open fields and a bank of trees next to the stream. The highest hill for miles around, Pire hill in the Staffordshire town of Stone is named after the pyres and beacon fires once built upon it.

But that night there were no beacon fires to light her way. She was alone, uncertain. The road ended in darkness, the line of street lamps

157

not reaching that far. She arrived a matter of seconds after the man. But he was nowhere in sight. Her dog suddenly went wild, yelping and barking at something unseen. She tried to calm him, but still he was frightened and agitated.

He was gone. He had not entered one of the last houses. Either he had continued up the pitch-black lane or had crossed the similarly dark field. But either way he had disappeared!

She heard only the wind as she strained to peer up the lane and across the fields. No-one. No footsteps of a man or his dog. Suddenly she was afraid. Home was only a short distance. She pulled at her dog's lead and hurried back along the lane.

That night she had a dream of the strange figure she had seen that evening. She was following him, the tall, dark figure in a cloak and wide-brimmed hat. He carried a staff. She went after him as he walked, slowly but assuredly pacing through the rooms of the old building.

Suddenly he turned. His bearded face was strong featured and knowing. *Pastor John*. The words came to her, burning into her dream memory. She knew it meant something of importance.

Carol Taylor, a friend of Martin's, did not know that that night she had witnessed a bizarre, supernatural event.

The road was much like any other, a close of semi-detached houses and bungalows in a suburb of the main town. It was 10.35 p.m. He rounded the corner and walked into the road, lit by two streetlamps. Lights from behind the house curtains told him the owners were not yet asleep.

As he walked he saw the man, a tall figure coming towards him on the opposite footpath. It was unusual to see a man so tall, about six foot four. Beside him was a dog, a black dog.

He walked on, taking no further notice. The man looked at him, a slow and determined movement of the head. His appearance was strange. A long black cape reached just below his knees, and his black hat was too wide brimmed. The man paced on, drawing level with him on the opposite side of the road. Again he looked, an unnervingly deliberate stare across the tarmac.

Martin began to feel nervous. There was something wrong, he knew it. Who was this stranger, this tall, peculiarly clad figure walking along the road near his house?

Instinct told him it was no ordinary man. He could not explain the inner feeling he experienced. Fear, yes, but not terror. An intuitive knowledge that what he saw was not as it should be.

The figure reached the streetlamp on his side of the road. For the third time his head turned, lifting slightly as it did so. Now Martin could see his face. A surge went through him, a rush of adrenalin, his body unconsciously preparing him for what was to come.

The face was a black, empty mask. Neither he nor the dog made a sound as they walked.

His nerve broke. Never had he moved so quickly. Looking back he saw the figure turn for a fourth and last time.

In seconds he was home, his heart thumping as he bent forward, gulping air as he stood outside the house. But why had he run? He *knew* the figure was not real, an apparition, a ghost, but surely he should have stayed and watched, gone over to it? But no. Never before had he experienced a psychic vision, and even investigators get scared!

That night he slept well, untroubled by the experience. He knew it had been a vision, in retrospect something he should not have feared, but for him to have such a vision .... it must mean something.

Carol and Martin compared notes. What they had both seen was clearly the same. Martin had been leaving Carol's house after visiting her brother, when she happened to mention a strange, dark figure she had seen on Pirehill Lane.

Quickly he asked her to say nothing more, and for the first time revealed what he had seen. Carol's subsequent description tallied exactly. *Pastor John.* The mysterious figure remained an enigma, but in some way Martin knew the man had a part to play. Somewhere, somehow....

★ ★ ★ ★

In early February Gaynor said that the search for the next four Lights must soon start. Again she was unable to undertake the search herself, but three others were available: Andy, Graham and Martin.

On Saturday, 5 February, the three travelled to Marion's to collect the Stone. *En route* they all received psychic information, the *guide* advising them that they must go to the Devonshire town of Crediton.

The process of releasing the fifth and sixth Lights was to be identical to the first four. However, the seventh and eighth would be different. To release them they would have to prove themselves worthy by passing a test, but they would learn no more of this until they had succeeded in finding Lights five and six.

Driving through the night they travelled south-west towards Devon. The sun was rising as the winding road passed through open fields and pastures, broken by low hills and grassy vales. The sign came into view as the road dipped into the shallow valley. *Crediton*.

In the early afternoon they made their way to the abbey, the town's central feature. Even as Dorchester Abbey had been important in their search for the First Light, so might the abbey in Crediton also hold the key to the Fifth Light.

Crediton Abbey is large and impressive, a medieval building of delicately ornate stone. As Andy examined a statue near the altar Martin and Graham walked through the cloisters discussing how they might find the person who would lead them to the *guardian*. To their surprise a large dog suddenly appeared from the vestry door and bounded up to them. Within seconds a bearded clergyman, dressed in a black cassock and carrying a wooden staff, followed the dog out of the vestry.

They were amazed. He was so similar to Martin's and Carol's visions of the *Pastor John* figure that it was beyond belief. They had both seen the pastor figure before, and this clergyman, the unwitting guide to the Fifth Light, was dressed exactly as they had seen him.

As Martin stared in disbelief, Graham bade him good afternoon to divert his attention from Martin's surprise. He *had* to be the one, but what mythical creature had he spoken about? Suddenly they knew. During their conversation he had made continued reference to his dog, saying that he was called Temujin, Genghis Khan's former name before he became Genghis Khan in 1206. The dog, was this the connecting factor? The black dog Carol and Martin had seen accompanying the pastor. But how was this an indication to the *spirit guardian*, a black dog? On the signpost near the Abbey they saw the name 'Black Dog'. Perhaps this place name was the link. The black dog must surely be their clue to the Fifth Light.

In the car Martin and Graham told Andy what had occurred, and he agreed that the small village they were heading for was undoubtedly the place.

Black Dog — a curiously named village — is small and quaint, a quiet cluster of homesteads seven miles north of Crediton. In the village centre stands an inn of the same name.

They sat in the lounge, discussing the events over a pint of beer and pub lunch. In legend a black dog is said to haunt the village, and especially the inn in which they were now sitting. As they talked they decided that the pub itself was probably on the sacred site for which they had been searching. There was now no visible evidence, no standing stone or burial mound, to confirm that it was once revered by the Megalithic culture. But, perhaps, many thousands of years ago, the small rise upon which the modern building now stood was on such a site.

They were convinced that this was it. They summoned the *spirit guardian*, the black dog, and as they did so a black labrador walked slowly and deliberately from the bar, through the connecting door and into the lounge, purposefully walking straight under their table to Graham. As he patted the dog he felt the now familiar energy running through him.

They had the Fifth Light! How these startling coincidences worked or were brought about was unfathomable. But what they could not deny was what had happened. The Fifth Light was now released back into the Meonia Stone.

The Sixth Light was at, or near, Lydford Gorge, about twenty three miles away. But that was all they knew.

In Anglo-Saxon times the Devonshire village of Lydford was a fortified borough with a mint. A monument to its history is Lydford Castle, once a prison for offenders against the special laws of the

161

forests and the stannaries. Built in 1195, the stone tower is set back from the road on an earth mound, next to which is the parish church, a fifteenth-century building constructed mainly of granite and surrounded by a half-overgrown graveyard.

After they had booked in at the Castle Inn, a small hotel adjacent to the old prison, they examined the building and discussed just how they were to find the physical guardian to the Sixth Light. Returning to the hotel still undecided, they settled for a drink and a game of darts. In the hotel lounge Graham had the strong psychic impression of monks chanting in Latin, followed by the sound of a cock crowing.

Next morning, after breakfast, Andy and Graham happened to speak to an elderly gentleman in the lounge. As they talked, Martin experienced *déja vu*, the feeling of something having happened before. Although he *knew* this man was their unwitting guide, he kept his mouth shut.

Without being prompted he then told them of a legend about a spectral cockerel that was supposed to act as guardian to an ancient earthwork on nearby Brentor. Brentor is an unmistakable landmark 1,130 feet above sea level, where, on the top of the tor, stands St. Michael's church, built between 1140 and 1150 A.D. It is a small but impressive building perched high above the surrounding plain. Legend has it that the church was originally planned for the foot of the hill, but when the bricks were continually and unaccountably moved from the base to the summit the mystified builders relented and erected it at the top. Around the base of the hill is a massive Pre-Roman earthwork, encompassing the whole tor.

It was ten thirty as they parked. Crossing the road they stood at the wooden gate, where the rugged track began its winding way up the tor to the church. That morning the scene held an air of foreboding. Drenched in swirling white mists the church stood out ominously against the sky. The path led away before them, rising gently onto the rocky slopes of the tor. The morning was cool and fresh, the sky cloud-covered and heavy with mist. After about a hundred yards the muddy track petered out to become a footpath, rising steeply towards the church. A light drizzle began to fall as they climbed, causing them to slip on the sodden grass. Finally they made it to the summit.

Although small, its sentinel-like position on the otherwise bleak tor made it all the more imposing, the church looking out over western Devon and eastern Cornwall, an almost flat plain receding to the distant horizon in all directions.

They entered the church. Andy read out the Latin words Graham had heard the monks chanting. Perhaps they held the clue to exactly how and where they must summon the cockerel guardian. Nothing happened. Perhaps they would find the words written somewhere in the church. They explored the interior, examining the benches and even the altar. Checking in the bell tower Andy found them, inscribed on one of the bells. But what did they mean? Graham went outside to ponder. As Martin flicked through the guidebook he came upon information about the bell. This was the Latin, translated into English. *I am called the cock, and I alone sound above all.*

He told Andy and then ran from the church to find Graham, who was looking out over the plain. They hurried back inside, knowing now that it was in the church itself where they must call upon the guardian cockerel. The three of them faced the altar. Above it was a stained-glass window depicting St. Michael.

They summoned the guardian. As Graham felt the energy surge through him and enter the Stone, Martin, standing only a few feet away, also experienced the almost surreal sensation of the energy reverberating through his body. Simultaneously he recalled a dream of weeks before which, at the time, he had dismissed. A figure in a stained-glass window exactly as he now saw the figure of St. Michael in the East window above the altar.

As they left the quiet church they heard the unmistakable crowing of a cockerel breaking the mid-day silence.

They had the Sixth Light.

Back at the car Graham had the impression of three circles that held the key to the Seventh Light. Andy recognised them as a series of three stone circles called the Hurlers, on Bodmin Moor. They drove from Brentor and across the county border to Cornwall. A cart track leaves the main road outside Minions and leads to the stones. Legend claims that the Hurlers are petrified men, punished for playing games on the Sabbath. Dated between 2,200 and 1,400 B.C. they are roughly the same size, about forty yards in diameter, and run in a near straight line north-east to south-west.

The rain beat down from darkened skies overhead as they crossed through the bracken. Within minutes they were soaked, their clothes sodden and dripping as they entered the first of the three circles. For some reason they felt they should each stand in one of the great stone rings. As they did so Martin had the impression of a lake. Simultaneously Graham heard the guide telling them they must go to Dozmary Pool. As they left the circles they were confused. This light was different from the others. They had been told it would be so, but now they had nothing at all to go on except that they knew they must walk to Dozmary Pool, a lake at the heart of Bodmin Moor. They returned to the car and drove the hundred or so yards to the nearby Cheesewring Hotel.

As they sat in the lounge debating their next move, the guide to the Light mentally instructed them that the test they must pass was to walk to Dozmary Pool nearly seven miles away. The realisation of what this would mean quickly struck them. To walk so far by night meant crossing the treacherous bogs of the moor, through the bitterly cold and dangerous moorland. There was no question that, with their inadequate clothing, such an expedition might prove disastrous.

Having decided to undertake the hazardous journey in the dark they prepared to face the consequences. Then, as they made their decision, both Martin and Graham felt a sudden overwhelming energy shoot through them.

To their surprise they had the Seventh Light.

It was followed almost immediately by a second wave of power. They also had the Eighth Light! They were astonished to find that their actions had released the Seventh and Eighth Lights simultaneously, both of which had been at the Hurlers Stone circle. They had no idea why this should be, but there was no mistaking the surge of power associated with the release of each Light. They had to assume they had passed the test to prove their strength of purpose in seeking the Lights. Perhaps it was this dedication which had acted as the trigger to release the Seventh and Eighth.

One Light remained, the last and most important, the Ninth Light that would bind the eight now held within the Meonia Stone.

In the following weeks both Terry and Gaynor received psychic impressions about the Ninth.

To release it involved a different procedure. There would be no guardians. Before they could release it they must first prepare the Eight Lights already within the Stone. To do this they would again have to visit the Avebury stone circle. They must go there on May Eve, the night of Beltane, one of the old Celtic fire-festivals and traditionally a day of supernatural power. At Avebury they would know what to do.

★　★　★　★

April 30, 1981 — Beltane

The day dawned, warm and sunny. Terry, Gaynor, Marion, Martin and Graham drove towards Avebury. Gaynor had told them that it was essential for five of them to go and release the last Light. They did not have to be there until around nine thirty.

Darkness had fallen as they drove down hill through West Kennet village, turning right onto the minor road leading towards Avebury. Here a stretch of the Avenue still survives, running parallel with the road, before it reaches the high embankment and enters the village.

Parking near the church they left the car and walked into the circle. By day the monument is visited by hundred of curious tourists; by night the silent stones lie alone and undisturbed. Their first sight of the huge standing stones was made all the more awe-inspiring in the near darkness. They walked round the outer embankment, talking only occasionally, five silhouettes against the dark horizon. The ditch below was a black shadow, the only illumination being the warm house-lights of the village. Crossing the road they again mounted the embankment, aware that they were making a deliberate trek clockwise about the high ridge. How long it took they did not know, but after an uneventful walk once round the circle they crossed the ditch and up the opposite side onto the central plateau of the henge.

Hardly a word had passed during their walk. Suddenly Terry broke the silence.

'Good Grief!' he cried as a blinding light burst around them, an aura of brilliant blue light shining brightly from their bodies, a luminous flare enveloping them all. They all saw it, the halo of power encompassing them. For over a minute the aura remained, shimmering and pulsating. Then suddenly it disappeared.

Instinctively they had done what had been intended. Only months later did they discover that to walk clockwise round Avebury is said to induce a sense of harmony with the natural earth energies of the circle. (1) By carrying the Stone round the outer embankment they had created the energy effect of the blue aura.

And then they knew. The eight Lights already in the Stone had been activated. Gaynor had the psychic impression that they must now go to the Uffington White Horse. There, at dawn the following morning, they would release the Ninth Light.

It was nearly midnight as the car headlamps bounced along the deep furrows of dried mud on the Ridgeway near Wayland's Smithy. Pulling off the road they drove a short distance and stopped on the ancient track. It was too late to book in to an hotel, and if they had to be up for the dawn it would not be worth it. They would sleep in the car. Marion, Gaynor and Terry stayed in the relative warmth of Terry's car, while Martin and Graham took the opportunity to see Waylands Smithy at dead of night.

As they approached, the wind swayed the many beech trees that encircle the barrow. By night the chamber is quiet and mysterious. Looking out over the land below they wondered what the dawn might bring. Gaynor had said they must go the the White Horse, 'the place of the dragon', as she called it. Christian legends state that the Uffington White Horse is a representation of the dragon slain by St. George on Dragon Hill, a flat-topped hill in the vale below. She had, many months before, told them that the secret of the Meonia Stone would only be known once the true significance of the dragon-slaying legend was understood.

★   ★   ★   ★

Dawn.

They walked in single file to the fort and stood above the horse. The land below stretched for miles, rising and falling gently to the distant skyline, a green plain dotted with homesteads and small villages. As the pale morning swept away the night, and a new sun spilled over the horizon, they felt an inner calm and strengthened power as the Ninth Light seeped from the earth into the Green Stone.

The transformation was complete. An energy that had lain dormant for thousands of years was once again awakened, returned to the Stone from which it had been taken so many centuries before. The power to slay the dragon was returned to the Meonia Stone.

166

Chapter Sixteen

Psychic Attack

By THE summer of 1981 life had returned to normal for those involved. Nevertheless, they hoped that in time somebody would receive a psychic impression telling them what they must do next now they had the Lights. But no message came.

In an attempt to learn something Alan and Graham travelled to the Sunderland's home a couple of times, but again nothing happened.

No messages. They began to wonder if, by releasing the Nine Lights, their job was finally finished. But no such luck.

One evening at Oaks Crescent something very disturbing happened. During a house party at Graham's flat a friend of Jane's, who knew nothing of the strange events, complained of a distressing feeling that something was very wrong in the house. Jane and Graham asked her to elaborate, but the girl, Karen, was unable to say more. All of a sudden she said she felt dizzy, and, without warning, collapsed onto the floor. Thinking she had perhaps had too much to drink, Graham and Jane helped carry her into the bedroom. They were followed by her girl friends, who wanted to call a doctor.

As she lay on the bed her friends gathered round. Suddenly she shot upright, and, ignoring everyone else, glanced in turn at Graham, Martin and Jane. A smile came over her face as she spoke.

'I am above you all,' she said, in a menacingly slow and deliberate voice, still grinning, '*You cannot win*'.

With this her face dropped and she fell back and began to sob. Jane and Karen's friends tried to comfort her, while a dozen others stared on in amazement. Finally she recovered. When questioned she remembered nothing. As Jane continued to calm her Graham and

167

Martin tried to smooth things over saying they had no idea what she meant. Secretly, they feared the worst, remembering the girl in Alan's office.

Next day Graham questioned Jane. As far as she knew Karen was perfectly normal, in fact, at one time, she had been a policewoman. Neither of her two friends had ever seen her behave so strangely as she had that night.

In the afternoon Karen returned to Oaks Crescent with one of her friends and begged for an explanation of what had happened. Eventually Graham told her in order to pacify her. But she found it almost impossible to believe. 'Can I meet some of the others,' she asked?

So, on the following evening, Graham agreed to drive her over to see Marion, where they were joined by Alan and Terry. Without warning, Karen fell into the same unconscious condition and repeated the identical message.

David Matthews, a friend of Jane's and who also knew Karen, could not believe what he had been told, although he was convinced that Karen and her friends had not lied.

One evening he arrived at the flat and asked Graham for an explanation. Finding himself in an awkward position, Graham told him about some of the strange events, though playing down the affair as best he could.

'It's impossible. I just can't believe it' said David, shaking his head in bewilderment.

Graham apologised, 'Well, that's what's been happening to us!'

'I don't know about the others,' David continued, his concern showing, 'but Karen's a rational woman. Whatever happened to her is real, not supernatural.'

Graham could only repeat what he had said. But even as he was speaking there came a sudden crash from somewhere below the flat. The whole place shook. The two men froze.

'What the hell was that?' David asked.

Graham shook his head.

'What's below here?'

'The cellars,' Graham said. 'But it couldn't be there. It must have come from outside.'

They checked immediately but found nothing. Then, as they walked back into the front room, there was a second and louder crash, rising in pitch and followed by a dull thud. A low rumbling echoed through the cellar beneath them. There could be no doubt about it. It had come from below.

Neither man spoke. After seconds of tense silence the sound came again, as though a heavy object was being dragged along. The noise penetrated the whole flat. Neither of them had heard anything like it before. As Graham looked around, undecided what to do, David lay down and put an ear to the floor.

'It's definitely coming from the cellar,' he said. 'How d'you get down there?'

Graham showed him the trap door beneath the hallway carpet.

'Right. Let's take a look.' Graham hesitated, but David pulled back the carpet and lifted the panel. He fetched a torch from the kitchen as David clambered down into the darkness, refusing to accept that it had been caused by anything abnormal. Graham handed him the torch and followed him down the steps.

All was silent as the light lit up the whitewashed brickwork of the first chamber. There was nothing in the cold, empty room to account for the noise. David walked through the adjoining passage into the second, smaller chamber. Again he found nothing. The cellar was dark and empty. As they stood in the gloom the only sound to be heard was the irregular drip of water from a leaking pipe.

David's face expressed his fear as he realised that there was no explanation. 'Christ!' he said, 'Let's get out of here.' Quickly he turned, making for the steps. 'This is bloody madness,' he shouted, as he finally clambered out.

But his experience was not to end there. When David Matthews had walked into the cellars searching for an answer, something evil had temporarily attached itself to him. A short time later he was on holiday in Cornwall with his girl friend. The noises at Oaks Crescent were the last thing on his mind as the pair walked down a lonely country lane one evening. Suddenly something was before them, a white shape, an illuminated figure as tall as a man. Its flaming brilliance contrasted against the darkness as it flashed past them, an unseen force almost knocking them aside. Both saw it, and both felt something immeasurably evil. Whatever the strange figure had been it greatly unnerved him for many months. It now appeared that whatever force of evil had been unleashed it was not only confined to those directly involved.

Graham spent some days at Marion's, trying to find an explanation. He also disliked the idea of spending time alone in the Oaks Crescent flat. He asked why they couldn't again use the Stone to repel these attacks.

'Out of the question,' said Marion. 'We might misuse its new power. No. We must wait until the time is right.'

Although it seemed that the evil force could no longer use the living as its agents, it was now launching its power against all those involved, trying its damndest to break up and isolate the group. Gaynor insisted, however, that no harm would befall them and that Graham could safely return to the flat.

Two friends, Barry Jones, and John Lawley, visited the flat. Both knew something of the events involved, but had not previously shown any particular concern. At around nine thirty that evening, there was an unaccountable and sudden temperature drop that made it so cold they could see their own breath. The roaring fire did nothing to alleviate the unnerving condition. Without further warning all present began to feel so nauseated that they had to leave. The following day while at home Barry found his own kitchen full of a thick incense smelling smoke.

But things became worse at Oaks Crescent. The inexplicable cold periods continued, becoming more frequent and intense. Visitors found it almost impossible to stay in the place. At night Graham was continually awakened by strange bumps and knocks; nearly everyone who came to the flat experienced a feeling of oppression. Lesley Connolly, the tenant of the apartment above, also felt it in her own flat. Previously she had been objective about the strange phenomena in the flat below, but now she felt a sense of deep depression whenever she was home. Soon she moved out for good, and a new tenant moved in. He knew nothing of the strange happenings but once again in a very short time he also complained that it was impossible to stay in such an awful atmosphere.

One evening, towards the end of May 1981, Martin, Terry, Alan and Pat called at the flat to discuss the worsening situation. The now familiar coldness surrounded them. Such an intense feeling of evil accompanied the bitter cold that they could hardly stand it. Terry and Pat offered Graham a room in their house while he looked for another place and they urged him to leave immediately. But Alan was disturbed. He was convinced that the opposition was trying to oust Graham. With the large flat gone there would no longer be a common meeting place.

Finally Graham agreed to brave it out, but just before his visitors left a strange, unearthly sound like a whistled lament echoed through the house. He decided to accept Terry and Pat's offer and spend the night with them.

Jane McKenzie's house also became affected. Late one night Jean Bosicombe was awakened by the feeling that something was in her room. She sat up in bed, wide awake, and looked round as an eerie green glow appeared outside the window. She jumped up to investigate, but the light vanished.

Jane McKenzie was also wide awake when she, too, witnessed the same phenomena. This time, however, it happened during the day. She was in the kitchen washing up at about six fifteen in the evening, when suddenly she felt that someone was watching her. She turned, but there was no-one. The unpleasant sensation lasted for several moments, mounting until she almost decided to leave the house. Then came the light, a prolonged flicker of intense brilliance all round her. She stood shocked and silent for some moments after it had faded, trying in vain to find a rational explanation for the bizarre phenomenon. The peculiar event left her weak and exhausted.

At almost the same time Martin and Graham had been in the Oaks Crescent flat when they heard a loud crash in the front room. They raced in, but found nothing. Then a strong scent of perfume filled the whole flat which, about ten minutes or so later, gradually changed to the sickly smell of rotting meat. The stench became so overpowering they were forced to leave.

At last Graham decided to leave the flat and move into the spare room in Jane's house. If Alan's impression was correct, the opposition had succeeded in driving them from their headquarters. *Parasearch*, as an organisation, was finished.

But the psychic assault was by no means finished. To have driven them from their headquarters was only one of the objectives. Now it re-affirmed its efforts by terrorising nearly everyone involved. By mid-summer a woman known to Alan Beard had begun falling into a terrifying state, during which she appeared almost to be possessed. In this condition she would spit and claw at Alan, screaming abuse and warning him to break contact with the others in the group. She also made references to matters she could not possibly have known about.

Alan spent more and more time visiting the Sunderlands looking for reassurance. Gaynor and Marion assured him neither he nor this woman could come to actual harm, but they could still not risk using the Stone until the time was right. They believed that this was exactly what the opposition was hoping for.

Alan agreed, but then something happened that broke his spirit. Fears for his own safety and that of his friends became too much when the woman fell into a strange trance and attacked him even more violently. By remaining completely calm, he was able to prevent injury to either of them. But by then he decided he had no alternative but to end his inolvement with Terry, Marion and the others.

Following Alan's break with the group, Terry and Mike went to see Marion, hoping that something might be done to halt the attacks. With Fred and Gaynor they tried to tune in to the *White Lady*, but Gaynor felt so intense a feeling of evil trying to stop them that they were forced to give up.

But perhaps the most bizarre experience of all involved Penny Blackwill at her Staffordshire home. As she was sitting reading one hot summer afternoon there came a knock at the door. She suddenly felt an intense chill running through her body and knew at once that something was terribly wrong. Answering the door she was confronted by a figure who radiated malevolence, a tall man with sinister features, dressed completely in black. His shoes, his suit, his shirt and tie were all black. Staring right into Penny's eyes and speaking in a cold, emotionless voice he warned her to have nothing more to do with Terry and Alan. As she stood dumbfounded, he turned and left without further explanation.

Immediately she phoned Terry who told her to call the police. But she protested, saying how could she possibly explain away his warning.

By the autumn Graham and Jane had broken with the group. One night Jane had woken, experiencing the fear that someone was in her room. She turned on the light but found nothing. She began to grow cold, then, to her horror, she felt cold fingers gripping her throat. After a few seconds of frantic struggle the feeling passed. The following day she felt so ill she was unable to go to work.

By now Graham had resolved to leave Wolverhampton for good. As the bitter winter of 1981 drew nearer, Mike, Pat, Terry and the

Sunderlands were, for the time being, all that remained of the group. The various forms of terrifying experiences had been too much for many of the others.

The next attack now concentrated on the Shottons. Pat felt an ever increasing feeling of hostility in the household, and every so often and without warning the sensation of acute panic. One day Terry was driving their daughter home from school when a man in another car appeared to swerve deliberately towards him and forced him off the road. Terry was petrified; it had followed a psychic impression warning him of just such an experience.

By October, the Sunderlands became very concerned by the strange phenomena that regularly plagued their telephone. Whenever they spoke to Terry the phone would cut out or emit mysterious electronic beeps and buzzes, making conversation impossible. Sometimes it would not work for days on end; at other times when it was working Terry was unable to get through. He would hear the ringing tone but there would be no answer. The G.P.O. was asked to investigate, but could not discover anything wrong. The possibility of visiting one another was made doubly difficult. Fred had no car and Terry's continually developed mysterious faults whenever he set out to travel to North Wales.

The Sunderlands were almost completely isolated. No attack had yet befallen them, although Marion was positive that the opposition was preparing to launch its final assault against the holders of the Stone. She knew that it was now time to act. They must prepare for battle with their nameless opponent.

Chapter Seventeen

Confrontation

W HEN Alan Beard travelled to the Shotton's Staffordshire country home on the evening of Friday 2nd October, he was more confident than he had felt for some time. He remained concerned that the frightening episodes which had plagued his life might resume once he again became involved, but Marion's insistence that both she and Gaynor had received fresh psychic messages gave him new hope.

Graham also felt optimistic as he joined Alan and Marion at Terry's and Pat's house. Having been out of touch for some time neither of them knew quite what to expect. When they arrived Marion explained the content of the psychic impression she and Gaynor had received. She was convinced of the importance of a remote pond some miles across the fields to the west of Saverley Green.

Some months before, many of the psychics had sensed its protective influence. They had found it after Pat had recognised the description. For many years, since her childhood wanderings in the countryside around Saverley Green, it had held an almost mystical attraction, as she had sat alone, quietly thinking, on a grassy knoll beside the water.

When she had gone there with Marion, Janet, Gaynor and Martin in the spring, something had happened which convinced them all that there really was something different about the place. As they stood admiring the scene, Marion felt a strong presence nearby. 'I am sure,' she said, 'that if we concentrate the influence will make itself known.'

And while they concentrated a great rush of wind on the calm, sunny afternoon howled around them. Janet, who was standing on the knoll, suddenly felt a surge of energy tingling through her body, and was nearly blown from the rise, which Marion later said was the centre of the power.

Marion was emphatic that the knoll could offer them the protective power they needed. Pat supported this belief. They both felt that a message awaited them.

They decided to sit in a circle and try to tune into the message. As they sat, the atmosphere changed; before long they began to receive pieces of information that formed the complete message.

A great protective force was going to be made available to them: a form of spiritual energy that flowed through the countryside. The gate to this power was to be opened to them that night, as it had been in the distant past. Just as *The Nine* had previously used it. To witness the phenomenon they must go outside and they would see. Terry and Alan went into the back garden to watch while the others remained seated in a circle. The time was 1 a.m.

In the darkness of Terry's garden the two men waited, looking out over the dark fields in the direction of the pond. All was quiet. Hardly a breeze blew and the sky was clear, the stars bright above them. Just as they were about to return indoors they head a low and distant rumbling. As the noise grew louder, from the direction of the pool there came a great, blue flash lighting up the whole horizon. Then there was silence. No sound, no light, just the eerie hoot of a nearby owl. They ran inside and called the others, but although they waited for over half an hour nothing more happened. Both were sure it had not been thunder and lightning. Firstly, it looked and sounded quite different; the rumbling had lasted much longer than normal thunder, and, secondly, the flash had occurred after the rumbling had started.

When they resumed the sitting Pat felt that the force had been successfully awakened. Now they must wait. Later they would be told more.

The following day Terry and Graham took Marion home, and were joined by Mike and Alan. Once more they sat in a circle, and this time Fred was also with them. Gaynor was in bed. Not long afterwards she came downstairs and told her mother that she felt her Lady in White was trying to tell her something. They let her sit with them for a short time, but almost at once she seemed to fall asleep on the couch. Marion and Fred tried to wake her, but she failed to respond. Then, as they began to get worried, Gaynor suddenly opened her eyes and sat up.

She appeared dazed, but then she said:

'I can't explain it, but all at once I found myself on top of a hill. I was standing beside an oak tree with an opening running through the base of its trunk, and my Lady in White was beside me. She told me that this was where we would find the power to overcome and destroy the evil.'

Terry and Marion then surprised the others by telling them that the previous night they had both dreamt of a single oak tree, but neither had mentioned it to anyone. Marion reminded them of the drawing Gaynor had made almost two years before, the sketch of the hill with a single tree on the side, which she had felt was certainly involved with their final task. Before they left that night Gaynor told them that her Lady wanted them to meet again at Terry's on 12 October, to prepare for something which would take place on the 13th, the anniversary of the fall of the Templars.

On Monday 12th, Marion, Gaynor, Graham and Alan met again at Terry's and Pat's. Alan was joined by Trevor Johnson, a friend who had expressed interest. For months he had been telling Alan of a series of dreams and psychic impressions he had had, all linked with what was happening. They sat in a circle awaiting further developments. One or two of them picked up a name, 'The Mount', and Marion said she was positive they must go there that night.

But where was it? Terry suddenly felt it was somewhere near where Penny lived, so they took out a map and studied the area. It was not long before they found the spot, a remote hill, marked 'The Mount', about two miles south of the tiny Staffordshire village of Bishops Wood.

Gaynor said: 'We *must* go there tonight', yet nobody liked the idea of travelling thirty odd miles to meet the unknown at the dead of night. However, she insisted, saying they would be shown something of great importance. So they relented and agreed to go, but Marion said that Gaynor must remain behind.

They set off in Terry's car. There was a full moon in a cloudless sky. The night-time country landscape was brighter than any of them could ever remember seeing before.

When they arrived at The Mount they followed the narrow lane leading almost to its summit, and when they saw the single oak tree standing out on the horizon they knew that this was indeed the right place.

They parked the car and climbed over the gate that led to the grassy field where the tree stood, alone and ominous in the silver moonlight. Drawing near they saw that the old, gnarled oak was exactly as Gaynor had described, with a large hole running through the base of its broad trunk.

For a time they walked about aimlessly, until Marion said they ought to link hands round the tree. As they did so, everywhere was silent. Even the light breeze dropped.

It was shortly after midnight: strange to remember that it was almost exactly two years earlier when the whole thing had started. So much had happened; so many lives had been changed. They had a few moments for reflection. They all knew it would not be long before they would be called upon to confront openly the force of pure evil itself.

Suddenly their reveries were broken by a dull rumbling sound. The whole ground appeared to be vibrating, alive with some unimaginable energy. None of them could account for it. It even crossed their minds to run, until Marion urged them to remain with their hands linked together round the tree. The noise stopped and it was silent again. For some moments they heard only their own breathing. They could almost hear their hearts pounding in anticipation. The soft breeze blew once more. All had returned to normal.

Then the impressions came to them. Somewhere below in the moonlit countryside was the place of immeasurable power. They could just make out the tiny wood at the foot of the hill as they left the tree and walked to the top of The Mount, the highest point for miles around. There, beside the copse below, they knew were the ruins of an ancient monastic building — White Ladies Priory. They already felt that it might hold the secret. The name itself, could it be coincidental? White Ladies! Penny had told them she had long believed that there they would discover their answer. Now they felt sure. The final secret awaited them at White Ladies Priory.

When they got home again they discovered that at the precise moment they had stood round the tree, Gaynor and Pat had been waiting anxiously when a great wind howled outside, and they had both felt a strong presence enter the front room. Gaynor told them that White Ladies Priory stood near the place they sought. When studying the map they could see the wood marked next to it, with a small stream passing through. They were positive that this was the place of the final secret of *The Nine*, the ultimate power to overcome the force of evil. But what was there? What was this place?

For some time many of them had believed that they would eventually discover a place of great power. Gaynor, Marion, Alan, Terry, Pat and Penny had all experienced vivid dreams of a grassy earth mound somewhere in a wood which they had felt to be near the centre of England. They had no idea what it was, but there had been many speculations. An ancient tomb? The tomb of Gwevaraugh or even an Egyptian princess? Perhaps the secret vault in the mystical tradition of the Rosicrucians? Whatever it was, it was there in that small area beside White Ladies Priory.

By early November there was nothing new to report. No further psychic messages. Gaynor and Marion told them they must have patience and wait for the right time. To their relief the psychic assaults had ceased since the blue flash behind Terry's house.

One Sunday early in November they decided to visit the White Ladies site to see if they could learn something more about it. The wood stands about fifty yards from the ruined priory, and a public footpath cuts through it to nearby Hubbal Grange. As they followed the pathway they noticed to their right a peculiar mound about six feet high and fifteen feet wide, running along beside the path for about fifty feet. All the trees upon it were dead. After examining it for some time they decided that this must be the place they were looking for.

Alan, Terry, Marion, Gaynor and Peter Marlow had arrived first, and were joined later by Trevor and his wife. As they examined the area, Terry, Alan, Marion and Gaynor experienced a great despondency. When they tried to explain the feeling to Peter and Trevor, Gaynor suddenly burst into tears. She said she could stand it no longer, and returned to the car with Alan and Marion.

Shortly afterwards Graham arrived with Andy Collins and two friends, Lynne and Dave, who knew something about the story and wanted to visit the place. None of them had been told what Gaynor had felt. As Graham and Andy talked with the others, Lynne and Dave wandered along the path to look at the mound. A few moments later they hurried back. Lynne was in tears and Dave was shaking. They had been standing on the mound when all at once they had felt the most awful sensation of depression, a kind of oppressive, black nothingness.

When Penny Blackwill arrived some time later with her friend Joyce, she too felt that there was something very wrong about the place and refused to stay for any length of time.

Everyone had expected it to give out a friendly atmosphere; instead it stank of depression.

What was it about the mound? Although the trees on it were dead, to those who had not tuned in it seemed to be a pleasant, grassy place in a lovely country setting, a babbling brook and the ruined medieval priory nearby.

In the weeks that followed a number of other psychics visited the spot and felt the same sense of melancholy, although they had not been told what others had experienced. As the weeks passed the feelings became even more acute, and people who had never before received psychic impressions began to undergo the same inexplicable depression at the site. Something terrible was happening there. But what? What *was* this place of such spiritual darkness?

The uneasy silence continued as the winter drew on, with still no sign of psychic messages. Gaynor and Marion felt that a great battle was near at hand, when they would have to confront the nameless evil opposing them. They knew they had no choice. But as time passed the waiting grew more and more tense and unbearable.

On Sunday, 17 January, 1982, the waiting was over. Marion phoned Terry and Alan and told them that they must drive over to see her that evening. Gaynor had dreamt of the White Lady again and she knew she had a message.

So, on that cold winter's day they journeyed to the Sunderland home, and, on Marion's instructions they — including Gaynor and Fred — sat in a circle to receive the message. Between ten twenty and midnight Marion had the following impressions.

'This is the time that the dragon shall be slain, the time for the destruction of the Evil One.' She wrote down the words as she heard them: 'You had to be brought together by me. No previous knowledge could help you.' And finally. 'The time is now.'

She said they must rest as much as possible between now and the thirtieth of January when they would again meet. And Graham must also be there. Finally, she had the impression that someone would be given a series of psychic instructions, but who would be the recipient and what these would involve was still unclear.

A day or so later Graham had a dream that was so unusual and vivid that when he awoke he recorded the details. Thinking how strange it was he telephoned Marion. She warned him that it was extremely important. He had dreamt that they were to construct a peculiar eight-pointed star, not simply a flat design but three dimensional. Its exact size, shape and colour he had remembered when he awoke.

When he had told the others of his dream, Trevor Johnson offered to build it for them, and a few days later the star was complete. It comprised two interlocking, three-sided pyramids, with each side just over three feet in length. The outside consisted of eight separate pyramids, each painted a different colour. Purple opposite yellow, blue opposite orange, green opposite red and white opposite black. On the inside it was covered in gold foil. What were they to do with it?

As they waited for the thirtieth to arrive no further instructions came. But something began to happen which caused them considerable alarm. It seemed as if the psychic attacks were about to be resumed.

It began at Terry and Pat's home one evening while they were watching T.V. The strong smell of a sweet perfume filled the whole house. Shortly afterwards the same occurred in Alan Beard's house, and then at the Sunderland home. But as they grew increasingly concerned Marion had the impression that it was, in fact, not an attack but some form of protection for what had to be done.

Saturday the thirtieth came without further incident, and Terry, Pat, Alan, Mike and Graham met at the Sunderland's Oakenholt home. As previously, they sat round a table in the living room and waited. After only a few moments Marion and Pat began to feel the familiar presence. Then they received a message which they were told was of the utmost importance. They were to prepare themselves for the coming conflict, a confrontation with the Evil One itself. It would take place on Monday 1 February, the festival of Imbolc, and the place for this final confrontation was to be White Ladies Priory. The grassy mound in the woods, where they had felt so much despair, was the *Place of Darkness*, where an almighty power could be summoned that would destroy the Evil One once and for all.

For centuries *The Nine* had known this, the final and most awesome

181

secret. They knew that only the full power of the Meonia Stone could be used to activate this *Place of Darkness*, and to summon a force so powerful that it could destroy not only any living soul but the evil they sought to oppose. Its might was so terrible that even the ancients had never dared invoke it. When the Stone was used and the gateway opened, those that were present must be protected otherwise they, too, would be annihilated. This protection would be given within the ruined walls of the Priory. Yet even this was insufficient. They must also make use of the protective power that had been opened for them at the knoll at Saverley Green on 2 October. It was here where the star they had constructed must be employed, as a means of storing the energy that would be made available to them.

Now they knew! Just after sundown on 1 February nine of them must go to the knoll and take with them the star. When they arrived they would know what to do. Then they must go to the Priory, taking the sword, the Stone and the star and when they arrived place the Stone on the grassy mound in the wood and quickly seek the protection of the Priory.

No-one liked the idea of leaving the Stone in the wood. It had not left their possession since they had found it. One of them — usually Gaynor or Marion — always had it with them. The message was repeated and they were told that the *Lady* herself would appear in order to use the Stone and direct its force against the Evil One.

Finally, before the influence left they asked their most important question. Who or what was the Evil One? There was no direct answer, except that should it appear it would assume the form of a massive bird of prey. Marion shivered, remembering the huge-winged abomination she had seen during her psychic projection to the Rollright Stones over two years before. They asked who should be there. They were told that Gaynor and Marion must be present. The others must be chosen.

For over an hour they sat discussing the situation. Should they go, perhaps to risk everything? To leave the Stone unguarded, to face the full power of the Evil One? There was no choice. They had already experienced something of its awful power. If they failed to stop it now, they would surely meet the fate of Mary Heath and the Order of Meonia.

They agreed to go. But who would make up the nine? They decided to postpone the decision until morning. The others left and Graham stayed overnight at Marion's. That night sleep came uneasily to all of them.

★ ★ ★ ★

The following evening Marion had taken her dog for a walk at about seven o'clock when she had the strangest feeling she had ever experienced. It was as if the whole world around her had become still and unreal, and she were no longer a part of it. The feeling left her as quickly and unexpectedly as it had come.

Then, at about one in the morning as she was about to go to bed, the feeling returned. She was sitting in a chair, talking to Graham, after Fred had gone upstairs. This time Graham also felt it. They stared at each other in amazement. Nothing moved — even the background ticking of the cuckoo clock faded into the distance. As they spoke their voices echoed as if through a vast, empty hall. Then, they both felt her enter the room, the familiar, reassuring presence of the Lady in White. They saw nothing, but they knew she was there. Suddenly they heard her voice, a soft, melodic whisper:

'I have given you a message of deception.'

As they looked around in disbelief the voice continued, but neither of them could quite hear what it was saying. It was weird, like the sound of sea breaking gently on a stony beach, mixed with the calling of gulls and the sound of the whistling wind.

Marion began to sway and fell back into her armchair. Soon she began to speak aloud the Lady's words. Graham hurriedly grabbed a pen and paper and wrote down what she was saying:

'The Evil One can often hear that which passes between us. I had the power to prevent this but he never knew. But as I speak to you now we are cloaked and screened from his senses.

At the Place of Darkness there exists a great force so terrible that for centuries none of us dared to release it. No-one has the power to control or direct it. The Meonia Stone holds the key to this force. With it the Dark Gate can be opened. Since the force released from the Place of Darkness cannot be directed to destroy the Evil One, he must be lured there in order to be destroyed.

There is a way to make him come. He knows that I do not have the power to open the gate without first becoming manifest, but should I do so he can then overcome me and destroy the Stone. In such circumstances the Stone can be destroyed. That is why I gave you the message to leave the Stone upon the mound. A message that he could hear. For now he believes that I intend to open the gate and try to direct this force upon him. Knowing that I will not have time to do this before he can destroy me, he will appear at that place to seek final victory over me and the power of the Stone. In this way he would be free for eternity.

When you stood upon the Mount I helped you to use the Stone to build the power at the Place of Darkness. The dark gate is now ready to be opened on this first day of February. I will use myself and the Stone as bait. But the power cannot be directed towards him until I have lured and brought him fully manifest to the Place of Darkness. The power you will then summon can destroy him. Marion, not I, shall use the Stone. You and the others now have the power to release the force from the safety of the Priory. You must open the dark gateway. He will not suspect anything. He does not know you have the power.

This communication is protected by my full power; he is not aware that I now speak to you. He is confident that the Stone will be placed upon the mound, and that I shall be there to use it.

Do not speak of this until it is completed, not even to each other. He cannot tell your thoughts unless I communicate normally to you without this protection, but he has the power to hear much of what you say.

Everyone except you must be made to believe that the Stone will be left at the mound. But you must only pretend to leave it there. Go through the motions, but keep the Stone with you. Then, when he manifests at the mound, Marion must use the Stone to open the gate so that the Evil One shall be destroyed for ever. You will all be protected in the Priory, but do not leave its walls until all is done. At the moment of confrontation you must find the extra protection by charging the sword with the power from the star. Graham must do this by thrusting the sword into the star. When you summon the force you will know what to do.'

The message stopped. Marion looked round. 'The protection is fading,' she said.

'Quickly,' Graham said, glancing at her. 'How will we know when it's safe to leave?'

'When we see the flashes of light indicating that the power is released. Either way it will then be over, for good or for evil.'

As the influence faded Graham asked her, 'But what about the White Lady?'

There was no answer. They knew that to make the Evil One believe the charade she, too, would have to be exposed to the power of destruction. She had made the decision to forfeit her existence in order to destroy him.

So this was it. Marion had to use the Stone to unleash a terrifying force from the *Place of Darkness*. Something so devastating that it could destroy not only the Evil One but the ones who called it forth.

The following day those who were to take part assembled at the Shotton home: Mike, Alan, Terry, Gaynor, Marion and Graham. In the short time left Terry had found three more volunteers to make up the nine. Chris Bourne, a close friend of his. A work colleague George Jackson, and his brother-in-law, John Goodwin. These three were eager to witness the strange events about which they had been told.

At 6 p.m. they all made their way to the grassy knoll in the fields behind Saverley Green to charge the star as they had been instructed. As they approached the spot the two stone gate-posts that marked the entrance to the small pond stood out like sentinels in the gloom. A bird fluttered from one of the small trees overhanging the water. Passing through the gateway they heard the stream that fed the pool. All was still. Only a faint wind blew across the fields.

Marion, Graham, Mike and Alan were the first to arrive. As she reached the knoll Marion felt a warm glow rising from it, a protective energy where they must place the star. The other three also felt it, a distinct heat spiralling from the ground below.

Placing the star at the centre of the rise they stood in a circle round it, waiting for something to happen. Nothing did. Nevertheless Marion felt it was done, and that the star was now charged with the protective energy they would need. They returned to the house for coffee. Marion and Graham said nothing about the previous night's message. The success of their mission rested on this secrecy.

At around eight o'clock Marion felt it was time to leave. In three cars they drove the thirty miles to the Priory. As they drew nearer the tension began to increase, an inner fear and the knowledge that they were preparing to face the evil itself. What horrors would the night hold? Would they be powerful enough to survive the confrontation?

Leaving the A5 they drove in convoy through the village of Bishops

Wood and along the small country lane that led to the Priory. Passing The Mount they saw the solitary oak tree. Now they were almost there. The headlamps threw light on the road ahead, illuminating the hedgerows on either side.

The narrow, mud lane leaves the main tarmaced road, a sharp right leading to the Priory and the mound, the *Place of Darkness*. As the cars bounced along the rough track the headlights cast eerie shadows on the rows of trees.

They were scared. The Priory was mysterious enough in daylight; by night heavy shadows cloak its four walls. They reversed the cars round, in preparation for a speedy get away should it prove necessary. They parked and stood on the furrowed lane. The cold night fell about them, nine huddled figures preparing to do battle with a force beyond their understanding.

Marion, Mike and Graham set off along the narrow pathway to the *Place of Darkness*. The night was heavy as Mike's torch shone back and forth across the mound, lighting up the dead trees and rough grass. Around them were more trees, a low rustling falling from the branches as the breeze brushed through them. The stream wound past the mound, a black ribbon on an already dark and forbidding landscape. Overhead the hurrying wisps of clouds broke to unveil the starry sky. A disquieting heaviness was in the air, an aura of oppression almost seeping from the mound before them. They were uncomfortable, scared. Marion moved forward and placed a stone on the mound, an object of the same size which Mike took to be the real Stone.

Hurrying away from the dark mound they joined the others and made their way to the Priory. The medieval building stands alone in an open field, a monument once alive and vibrant, now forlorn and deserted. The roof has long since collapsed, exposing the moss-covered walls to the mercy of the elements.

Silently they stood in the darkness. Waiting. Waiting in the confines of the ruined Priory, its stone walls surrounding them with a thousand years of untold history. The old ruins that once sounded to the solemn chanting of the long-departed Brides of Christ stood around them, dark and lamenting. The night was cold but calm, only a light and occasional breeze adding sound to the stillness.

Through the archway in the stonework they could distinguish the shapes and shadows of the surrounding countryside, ill-defined shadows that held unknown menaces. Darkness. Fear.

Seconds passed, but still no-one spoke as they stood, hands linked, in a circle. They glanced towards the star in the centre. The object they had built now seemed less familiar, more bizarre in that unreal setting at the centre of the circle, a multi-coloured, eight-pointed three dimensional star. Several of them glanced up, watching the clouds give way to occasional patches of dark sky studded with silent stars. Still their eyes were drawn back to the copse, looking through the arch towards the black woods. It was in that small copse that it would happen, the final battle that centuries of trouble, fear and death had sought to postpone until that night. Soon. Very soon. But now there was darkness, cold, unmoving. The intermittent gusts of wind blew through the naked branches of the tree surrounding the grassy mound resting in the centre.

It was so close, less than fifty yards away, their only protection the cold, stone walls of the Priory. All around was darkness. No lights, No houses. No-one.

Marion, who stood opposite Graham, broke the circle and held her right arm aloft, her fist tightly clenched. In their minds they reflected on the incredible and terrifying events which had led them here. The psychic messages, the sword and the Stone, the Order of the Meonia and the Lights. And now this, the final confrontation with the evil force that for years had opposed them. It was beyond reason and unbelievable. But it had happened.

The cry came from the woods. It sounded like a strange bird. They froze. No-one spoke. Could it have come from any ordinary bird.? The second screech swept away their hopes, a horrible, unnatural wail. Terry tried to speak, but quickly Marion silenced him.

The cry came again, nearer and higher, climbing skywards from the dark copse. Towards them! Terry, Alan and Graham broke the circle in fear. Again Marion pulled them back, shouting at them to stand firm. Then the noise was overhead, circling and swooping in the darkness, a sickening shriek seizing their minds and bodies with fear.

Marion shouted to Graham, 'Quickly, take hold of the sword.'

A terrible cry, like a woman in pain, rang through the cold night air above the copse. Again the screech from above, loud and long, diving onto their fragile circle below. It circled and fell towards them with a final, defiant screech as it receded into the woods.

187

The screech was followed by a dreadful howling. Marion threw back her arms and mentally summoned the power of *The Nine*, the Stone and the powers of all that is light and goodness to destroy the nameless evil that assailed them. At her command Graham thrust the sword into the star, a painful jolt coursing through his arms as the cold metal pierced the object.

A blinding light exploded from the wood, a massive flash tearing away the darkness, accompanied by an ear-shattering crash. Within seconds there was another huge flare. The landscape lit up for hundreds of yards, pure white light as bright as the sun. A second crash followed, as a third circle of light erupted into view and, for several seconds, hovered over the copse itself, almost blinding them with its brilliance.

Finally, a deafening cry tore through the woods as two spheres fused together, exploding like a thousand suns, and bringing an impossible daylight.

Then silence.

Marion burst into tears. It was finished. She knew they had succeeded. The destruction of the Evil One had been finally accomplished. They knew, indisputably, that they had triumphed in their fated task.

Hurrying away from the Priory they made for the cars, eager to escape from the cosmic battlefield. The age-old evil had been destroyed, totally and utterly, by the devastating power released by the Meonia Stone.

Later that night they sat huddled around the comforting fire in Terry's house as Pat listened to their story. Only Gaynor seemed undisturbed by the experience.

'Is that really it?' asked Alan, his voice still trembling. 'Is it all finally over?'

Gaynor lifted her head and smiled,

'For some of us,' she said, 'Perhaps.'

Reflections

LEAVING aside the overriding theme, the content of the psychic messages and speculation about what may have been happening throughout, we are left with an impressive chain of paranormal experiences. Each incident deserves far more space for discussion than is presently available. In all we have related no fewer than one hundred and thirty two experiences that would appear to be paranormal, fifty one of which were — as far as we can ascertain — objective physical phenomena. Anomalous, but nevertheless, real events very often witnessed simultaneously by a number of people.

There is, in fact, nothing particularly unusual about people claiming to have experienced such strange phenomena. Many are the reports of normal families forced to leave their homes because of poltergeist activity, of sane and responsible people attesting to the appearances of ghosts and apparitions. All over the country there are spiritualist mediums who fall into trance during which spirit beings purportedly communicate with the living. Sometimes we read about people seeing visions of the past, and even of archaeological discoveries aided by those with psychic gifts. (1) And not least of all, stories of close encounters with UFOs and their occupants often appear in the popular press. But what makes this particular series of events so remarkable is that so many different paranormal phenomena are interrelated.

There is only witness testimony to verify that these events took place. However, it is not merely a case of one or two close friends, or a small group of people from the same household, street, or office. In all forty six separate witnesses are mentioned by name in this book. People from all over the country: London, Staffordshire, Stoke-on-Trent, Wolverhampton and North Wales, most of whom came to know one another only because of what took place. Another aspect

189

which also makes it so unusual is that they have such diverse backgrounds, age groups and professions: municipal council officers, school teachers, law students, service men, ex-police personnel and a government tax inspector to mention but a few.

Very often the witnesses had absolutely no knowledge of what had previously been happening. Some knew a little, but more importantly were sceptical about the claims. In fact many of those who became involved had never had any form of psychic experience, or indeed ever witnessed any paranormal phenomena. For example, the strange phenomena that took place at the White Ladies Priory on 1 February 1982. Here there were nine witnesses, three of whom had had no previous involvement.

Regarding the paranormal experiences themselves, it is easy for us to comprehend — even if we cannot fully explain — some of the phenomena that have been outlined. However, we cannot even begin to conceive how it was possible that some of these ever happened. But, by the same token, we need to record what occurred, however incredible it might seem.

We could continue with other examples. But all we wish is to emphasise how impossible it becomes in trying to evaluate the story from a paranormal research or parapsychological perspective. We do not claim that this book is the result of paranormal *research*, although paranormal researchers were involved. We could have attempted perhaps such a work, and maybe others will undertake this task in the future. Now we wish to record only what actually happened. It would be unwise to venture further into the treacherous realms of conjecture while so many questions remain unanswered.

This incredible story story has *not* ended! Even as *The Green Stone* was completed the phenomena continued.

We have documented these later events as they happened, and are now preparing a second book covering these new developments.

October 1982

190

Notes

References quoted do not necessarily cite the original publisher or publication date, but are the editions consulted by the authors.

Chapter Two

1 The full account of the Avis Case was presented by Andy Collins and Barry King in the magazine *Flying Saucer Review* in two parts. *The Aveley Abduction*, F.S.R. Vol 23 No 6 and Vol 24 No.1: 1977.
2 Astral Projection, also called Out of the Body Experiences, is the strange phenomenon that many claim to have undergone, where they find themselves temporarily separated from their physical bodies.
3 For a fuller account of the Sunderland family experiences read *Alien Contact* by Jenny Randles and Paul Whetnall. Neville Spearman. 1982.

Chapter Three

1 *The Deeside Advertiser*, Thursday 4 October 1979.
  The Chester Chronicle, Friday 5 October 1979.
2 Photograph reproduced on page 45 of *Alien Contact*.

Chapter Four

1 Bury, Berry or Bery: A specialization of the Old English, Burh or Byrig, meaning an enclosed or fortified place, which still survives in many local names. *Oxford English Dictionary*.
2 Knights Templar suggested reading:
  World of the Crusaders. Joshua Prawer. Weidenfeld and Nicholson 1972.
  The Knights Templar. Stephen Howarth. Collins 1982.

Chapter Five

1 See: *Gunpowder Treason and Plot*. C. Northcote Parkinson, Weidenfeld and Nicolson. 1976.

2 Full English translation of the *Fama* made by Thomas Vaughan in 1652 begins on page 238 of '*The Rosicrucian Enlightenment*'. Frances A. Yates, Routledge and Kegan Paul. 1972.

3 Second Rosicrucian document known as the *Confessio*. Vaughan's full English translation begins on page 251 of *The Rosicrucian Enlightenment*.

4 Third Rosicrucian document known as the *Chemical Wedding*. An English translation made by Ezechiel Foxcroft in 1690 appears in *A Christian Rosenkreutz Anthology*. Paul M. Allen. Rudolf Steiner Publications (New York) 1968 as do Vaughan's versions of the *Fama* and *Confessio*.

5 For an objective study of the Rosicrucian mystery see: *The Rosy Cross Unveiled*. Christopher McIntosh, Aquarian Press. 1980.

6 See: *The Morning of the Magicians*. Louis Pauwels and Jacques Bergier. Granada. 1971.

Chapter Six

1 Confession of Thomas Wyntour in his own handwriting, now preserved at Hatfield House, the home of Lord Salisbury.

2 As an ancient Celtic fire festival, the 31 October is a day long believed to hold magical significance. Only in recent years has it become commercialised. There are eight such festivals: the solstices, equinoxes and half days of the Celtic calendar. The main four are Imbolc on February 1, Beltane on May Eve, Lugnasadh on August 1, and Samhain on November Eve. Samhain later became All Hallows Eve and thus Halloween. On the eight days the ancients believed that great magical power could be evoked, and modern-day witches still revere these days calling them Sabbats. For further information see: *In Search of Lost Gods (a Guide to British Folklore)*. Ralph Whitlock. Phaidon Press. 1979. pages 128-158.

Chapter Seven

1 For the St. George Parry see: *Teach yourself Fencing* C.L.de Beaumont OBE. The English Universities Press. 1968, pages 99-100.

2 For symbolic meaning of the Dragon and Dragon slaying see: *An Illustrated Encyclopaedia of Traditional Symbols*. J.C. Cooper. Thames and Hudson.1978.
   See also: *The Book of the Dragon*. Judy Allen and Jeanne Griffiths, Orbis. 1979.

3 In 1117, when the Templars were founded by St. Bernard of Clairvaux

and his cousin Hughes de Payens, nine selected knights were chosen
to spend nine years in Christian-occupied Jerusalem at the Temple of
Solomon, preparing themselves for the task of ruling the proposed
order of Knights Templar. Once again *nine* knights.

Chapter Nine

1 Although there had been no announcement proclaiming the existence of
   the Rosy Cross fraternity in 1605, in the previous year a lengthy
   manuscript entitled the *Naometria* appeared in Wurtemburg. Its author
   was a mystic and theologian named Simon Studion. Many who have
   examined the document, now in the *Landesbibliothek* at Stuttgart, believe
   that, amongst other indications, a rose cross design reproduced in its
   pages shows this to be the earliest known Rosicrucian document.
2 Or e such illustration can be found in the *Naometria*, and is reproduced in
   The Rosy Cross Unveiled.
3 See: *The Rosicrucian Enlightenment*, pages 1-29.
4 The appearance of the stars was recorded and commented upon by
   Johannes Kepler in his *De Stella nove in pede Serpentarii; De Stella incognita Cygni:*
   published at Prague in 1606. (See *The Rosicrucian Enlightenment*).

Chapter Ten

1 For information about the Rollright Stones and its connections with
   witchcraft see:
   A guide to Occult Britain. John Wilcock. Sidgwick and Jackson. 1976.
2 *Murder by Witchcraft*. Donald McCormick. John Long. 1968.
3 *See: An Encyclopaedia of Traditional Symbols*.
4 From Vaughan's translation of the *Confessio*.
5 It must be stated that the identity of any member of this witch coven still
   remains a mystery. One or two suggestions were made, but subsequent
   investigation negated these.

Chapter Eleven

1 *Automatic Writing* is where a person feels inspired to write without being
   consciously aware of what they are writing about. Many Spiritualists
   believe they can communicate with the spirit world in this way.
2 The story of Parsival, written by Wolfram von Eschenbach between
   1300 and 1310, refers to a magical green stone, and flatly declares that
   this stone was *the graal*. It would appear that the first ideas about the Holy
   Grail came about through the earliest *Arthurian Romances* referring to a

193

graal. The first to mention it is *Conte del Graal* written by Chrétien de Troyes. In this last of his five *Arthurian Romances*, composed probably between 1175 and 1190, he never states what a *graal* actually is. The word was not universally understood even in France during this period. (See: *Wales and the Arthurian Legend*, Roger Sherman Loomis, University of Wales Press, 1956).

Wolfram von Eschenbach, however, refers to it as *Lapsit Excillis*. This was taken to mean *Lapis Excilis* — a small stone.

The idea of the *graal* or grail being a chalice used at the last supper by Christ, came about thanks to the misinterpretations later popularised by Tennyson and Wagner.

Eventually, the *Lapis Excilis* became integrated into Alchemical ideas where it becomes associated with the so called *Philosopher's stone*.

Arnold of Villanova, in the 15th Century *Rosarium Philosophorum*, writes: *Hic lapis excilis extat precio quoque vilis spernitur a stultis, amatur plus at edoctis*. Literally translated: *This insignificant stone is indeed of trifling value, it is despised by fools, the more cherished by the wise.*

A legend of unprecise age stated that a small green stone, long considered to have been a talisman against evil, was believed to have fallen out of Lucifer's crown when he was cast out of heaven. Page 117, *The Grail Legend*, Emma Jung and Marie-Louise von Franz, English translation, Hodder and Stoughton. London 1971.

Also see: *The Quest of the Holy Grail*, Jessie L. Weston, Frank Cass, 1964.

Chapter Twelve

1 On Monday, 4 February, 1980, Andy and Graham reported the break-in to the local police, who took samples of the blue jelly for analysis and also made a cursory examination of the Flat. However, the results of the analysis were not forwarded to the investigators. With the police involved the story broke and an account of the week's events appeared as the cover story in the local paper: *The Wolverhampton Chronicle* of Friday 8 February. On Monday 11 February, a film crew from the Midland independent television network unexpectedly arrived at the flat and interviewed the witnesses. This was screened on the regional programme, *A.T.V. Today*, a few days later.

Chapter Thirteen

1 The spelling of *Mary*, as *Marye*, was probably due to the Gothic revival

popular during the second half of the last century.
2 Two giant sculptures of baboons in quartzite squatting on their haunches, are at Hermopolis in Egypt, the site sacred to the god Thoth.
3 By Akhenaten's time, during the New Kingdom, the winged disc was a symbol of protection inscribed above temple doors.
4 A pseudonym is used here since his relatives may still be alive today, having had no involvement in his Victorian black-magic practices.

Chapter Fourteen
1 Amon was the principal god deposed by Akhenaten.
2 See: *Magical and Mystical Sites,* Elizabeth Pepper and John Wilcock, Abacus, 1978. Pages 289-298.

Chapter Fifteen
1 See: Page 243 *Megaliths and their Mysteries,* Alastair Service and Jean Bradbery, Weidenfeld and Nicolson, 1979.

Reflections
1 *Psychic Archaeology,* Jeffrey Goodman, Wildwood House, 1978.

Appendix

The history of the Stone and the Nine

There are certain facts that deserve clarification about the historical periods mentioned during this account, in order that the psychic messages may be considered in their proper context.

In the course of the account, the Megalithic peoples have been mentioned on several occasions. The psychic messages received indicated that it was with these ancient peoples that the whole story had its beginnings. It was by their unwitting hand that the malific being, whatever it was, came into existence, and it was they who created the Stone as a means ultimately to destroy it.

So who were the Megalithic peoples? We have said that they were the race who constructed such monuments as Avebury and Stonehenge, but it is important to explain a little about this civilization. However, we are not historians nor archaeologists and are therefore only presenting information assimilated from subsequent research and reading. We have included notes for the more important reference sources used, and, in addition, there is a suggested reading list for those who may wish to read further.

The word Megalith, from the Greek meaning a great stone, is the term commonly used for any large stone structure erected in Western Europe from approximately 5000 to 500 B.C. However, the monuments erected after about 1400 B.C. are considered to have been the work of a markedly different culture. So the more popular term *Megalithic* (Civilization, Culture, Peoples etc), is the word used for the period in Western European prehistory from around 5000—1400 B.C.. It must also be mentioned that the term *Megalithic monument* is often found referring to constructions dating from this period that are not necessarily made of stone, such as earthworks or mounds. Finally it will save confusion to add that the term *Megalithic Age* is not an archaeological term, but a popular lay usage. The period between 5000 B.C. and 1500 B.C. in Western Europe falls into two distinct ages: The Neolithic (New Stone Age), and the Early Bronze Age. (1)

No contemporary records survived from the Megalithic period in Europe; in fact, none seem to have been made. No written accounts tell us what these extraordinary people thought, how they lived, what religious beliefs they may have held, or, most frustrating of all, why they built the thousands of mysterious monuments still to be seen scattered across the countryside.

Although some civilizations running concurrently in other parts of the world developed means of recording their history, the Megalithic areas were still, as far as we are concerned today, very much in a prehistoric era. The only indications of Megalithic culture come from the findings of archaeologists who painstakingly unearth and reassemble the belongings that these men and women in a far off time left behind. Ironically, it is often those discarded objects that provide us with an insight into their way of life. Unfortunately it can tell us little more than the bare fundamentals of daily life many thousands of years ago. In effect, it is like trying to understand someone today by the contents of their dustbin.

For centuries nobody had any idea how old these Megalithic monuments really were. The early Church considered them to have been built by the pagan Celts that they hoped to convert. The first antiquarians of the Renaissance took them back a little earlier, classical study revealing that the Romans had made written reference to them and their use by the Druids for sacrificial purposes.

Today, however, modern scientific techniques have shown that they are in fact very much older. The great sarsen stones of Stonehenge, for example, by no means the oldest Megalithic monument, precede the Roman invasion by as many years as there have subsequently elapsed since the time Julius Caesar set foot in Britain.

The dating of these prehistoric sites is achieved basically in three different ways, which after being interrelated and cross-checked with the findings at other sites give a reasonably accurate estimation of the age of many constructions of great antiquity.

First, what is known as the thermoluminescence present in pottery, found at or near the site in question, deteriorates at a fairly constant rate. This process begins once the pot has been fired, so the period that has expired since the time of the firing can be estimated. Second, plant pollen is able to survive for a great length of time, and after scientific analysis its age can be established. Pollen found in the right place can tell scientists when certain archaeological discoveries were deposited.

But the most widely used procedure is radiocarbon dating: organic matter, in whatever form, either animal or vegetable, contains Carbon 14. Once the living organism has died the Carbon 14 gradually decays until some 60,000 years later it disappears altogether. By a chemical analysis the amount of Carbon 14 can be gauged, thus making dating possible. Although the date the stones were erected cannot be ascertained, tell-tale organic remains can be dated. Very often organic debris is found beneath the stones and, fortunately for the archaeologist once again, what the builders discarded can serve an invaluable purpose. The tools employed by Neolithic man were frequently little more than modified animal antlers, or implements made from bone. Where these have been found, lining the bottom of the pit where the stone was placed, then they can be radiocarbon dated and the relative age of the site reckoned.

By using these methods the earliest Megalithic structures have been found to date from around as early as 4700 B.C., which is about 1700 years before the first Egyptian pyramids were built.

These earliest monuments of the Megalithic age are known as Dolmens, which are, in effect, stone chambers formed from upright stones with one or more large flat stones laid across them to form a roof. Originally many of them would have been covered with a mound of earth, but often this has been eroded leaving the stones bare and exposed.

The Megalithic ideas seem to have begun in Brittany or Portugal. Nor did it take long for the culture to spread throughout many parts of Europe. By 3600 B.C. it had reached the British Isles, where, for the following 1000 years, simple dolmens, earthen long barrows (such as Wayland's Smithy) and other variations of so-called chambered tombs dominate the period. The really fascinating and mysterious period in the Megalithic era began around 2500 B.C. About that time a great leap forward occurred, almost overnight, in archaeological terms.

In certain areas of Europe, in particular the British Isles and Brittany, the Megalithic peoples started to build staggeringly impressive structures and gigantic earthworks. There are many examples of an earthwork known as the Cursus, long, narrow enclosures, usually closed at both ends and formed by two parallel banks and ditches. Some run as far as six miles. There are also huge earthen mounds such as Silbury Hill near Avebury, which is 130 ft high and covers five and a half acres. And in many instances natural hills were the focus of gigantic reshaping projects, Glastonbury Tor in Somerset being the best-known example. Great stone rows, such as Carnac in Brittany, where hundreds of tall standing stones, some 12 feet high, cover many acres. And all over Europe thousands of solitary standing stones known as Menhirs were erected, some only a few feet high but others very much taller. The Great Menhir just outside Locmariaquer in Brittany, which today lies shattered on the ground in four huge pieces, once stood over 60 feet high.

But most enigmatic of all are the circles or rings of stone. Although there are a few isolated examples elsewhere in Europe, these appear to have been something of a British peculiarity. There seems to have been little or no build up to these. They began in a big way with structures such as Avebury and Stonehenge.

Just why this sudden leap forward came about is still uncertain, although it is thought to have had some connection with an influx of a new people — The Beaker people, so called because of the pottery which is characteristic of them. They came from Central Europe or perhaps Spain, and brought with them their new skills which caused them to be quickly adopted by the Neolithic communities who, one theory suggests, adopted them as a ruling priesthood. However, although the Beaker people undoubtedly brought with them a knowledge of metal working, there is much archaeological evidence to suggest that the move towards some of the grander structures had begun just prior to their arrival. The influence of the Beaker people on these mammoth undertakings seems to have been that of introducing a more centralised form of administration that made possible the organisation of the vast work forces necessary.

After about 2000 B.C. the work on larger stone circles in the

British Isles gave way to a great number of smaller ones of which about 900 are known in Britain and Ireland.

What extraordinary purpose lay behind these enigmatic constructions, built from 2500 B.C., remains open to controversy. The most conservative archaeologists claim that they were erected for some unknown religious purpose.

There seems to be little doubt now that many of the stones are aligned to the rising and setting of the sun on particular important days of the year. Some authorities hold to the belief that the fundamental purpose of the stone circles were as astronomical observatories at a time when for the greater part of the year the skies over Britain were far clearer than they are today. The purpose, they say, for this was to give the Megalithic peoples a means of accurately calculating dates essential for the relatively advanced farming procedures they had adopted. However, the sheer size of Avebury indicates very strongly that at least there was *some* ceremonial purposes intended here, besides merely that of observing the skies.

The purpose of the Cursus constructions and gigantic mounds like Silbury is perhaps more mysterious still. Numerous theories for the Cursus earthworks have been advanced, ranging from their use as ancient race courses ('Race course,' incidentally, is what the name coined by Dr. William Stukeley, an 18th century antiquarian, literally means) to the more probable theory of them being vast processional ways for seasonal fertility rituals. Silbury Hill, once thought to have been a huge burial mound, was made more mysterious when modern excavation conducted between 1968-70 found no evidence of any burial chamber at its core. The mystery surrounding these Megalithic sites has caused many diverse theories to have been put forward.

A one-time commercial traveller Alfred Watkins, in his book *The Old Straight Track*, written in the 1920s, describes how, during his travels through Herefordshire, he came to the conclusion that many of these ancient sites could be joined together by straight lines drawn on maps. This led Watkins to the conclusion that these supposed alignments, which he called ley-lines, were prehistoric trade routes. However, his theory is discredited by the fact that many of his ley-lines pass over such obstacles as bogs and cliffs. Yet the ley-line theory did not die.

201

In more recent years many have been inspired by the idea of a universal system of Megalithic sites. A number of writers have advanced the concept of ley-lines being not pathways but power lines, channelling some unspecified terrestrial energy utilized, or at least plotted, by Megalithic man. Author John Michell, more than any other, is chiefly responsible for the popularization of this idea. His book *View over Atlantis*, which discusses in romantic style the idea of these arterials of spiritual power, became very popular in the early seventies. (2) Archaeologists for their part, however, have not been over impressed by the ley-line concept. Most, it would seem, either totally ignore the theory or put these alignments down to pure chance. (3)

The idea that the great stones themselves contain some manner of psychic energy goes back a long time. However, archaeologist and respected psychic researcher T.C. Lethbridge brought respectability by pointing out that many people, himself included, are able to sense some electric-like energy emanating from certain Megalithic stones. (4) Perhaps the most interesting theory put forward in convincing style comes from the authority on dowsing, Tom Graves. In his book published in the late '70s, *Needles of Stone*, Graves advocates that there are channels of terrestrial energy running across the globe and that these are the acupuncture lines of the earth. Whereas the acupuncturist inserts needles into the flesh of a patient in order to heal the body, the Megalithic peoples inserted stones into the earth in order to improve their quality of life. (5)

Many other imaginative theories have been advanced to explore the purpose of the Megalithic monuments. Not least amongst them those putting forward the idea that in them we have evidence of extraterrestrial visitations. John Michell, for example, in his *The Flying Saucer Vision*, reproduces a picture of Stonehenge reconstructed from the Ministry of Works guide book showing how it would have originally looked from the air, suggesting that it appears like the popular representations of a UFO. (6)

Whatever the true purpose of the Megalithic monuments, one thing is certain about the people who built them. Archaeology has shown us evidence of an extremely organised and peaceful society, and a society, for its long duration, free from war. Their early monuments or communal gathering and living areas do not appear to have been fortified, (whatever the true purpose of the great ditch and earth bank at Avebury, archaeologists are certain that it was not defensive), and there is an absence of weapons suitable for anything other than hunting.

So what happened to this harmonious civilisation which gave way to the warring tribes that followed it? A trend that was to span the next three and a half thousand years. What brought about the end of the Megalithic culture which had lasted just as long?

In recent years scientists have been able to trace prehistoric weather patterns by studying the remains of animal and plant life discovered at sites of different periods. The result of this work has given a fairly comprehensive view of climatic conditions throughout this period. Between about 4000 B.C. and 1400 B.C. the weather in the British Isles and North Western Europe had been warm and fairly dry, (The Sub-Boreal period). However, about 1400 B.C. there was a dramatic change of climate, bringing about colder and wetter conditions which have persisted pretty much unaltered until the present day, (The Sub-Atlantic period).

This dramatic change of climate certainly created many changes in life style. Farming became more difficult and the relatively easy manner of living that gave them time to dwell upon more spiritual undertakings went with it. The onus was now on survival, and substantial dwelling sites became more desirable.

From 1400 B.C. onwards the great Megalithic constructions and stone circles were no longer built in Northern Europe and the British Isles. The Megalithic culture quickly gave way to what has become known as the Wessex culture, and the contents of the graves discovered from this period suggest the existence of a warrior *élite* unknown before this time.

The psychic messages, which originally began with the Joanna communications, told us that some of the last Megalithic people in the British Isles left this country and came eventually to Akhenaten's Egypt. As we have previously mentioned, since the first messages we have been able to discover that this could have been possible. The climate changed in Northern Europe between 1500 and 1400 B.C. and with it no more of the great Megalithic monuments were constructed.

Turning to Ancient Egypt, the task of tracing its history is considerably easier. Here there are hieroglyphic and other forms of writing that well record much of what took place. Dating is open to a small margin of speculation, but the Pharoah Akhenaten is generally considered to have lived and died somewhere between 1400 and 1350 B.C.

Apart from what the psychic messages told us, it is safe to assume that the select ruling priesthood in the British Isles around 1400 B.C. were looking on in dismay as their well-organised society rapidly crumbled and fell apart. No more great monuments or stone circles were built and those that existed fell into disuse. Presumably they must have been powerless to prevent the new warrior *élite* from taking over as the ruling body. A new type of aristocracy for a new age. The old priesthood could no longer offer the people what the new environment demanded that they require. Conditions had become harsher, people became more quarrelsome and what little could be scraped together was jealously guarded. The fertile areas were occupied and defended against others who might be less fortunate. Separate tribes quickly sprang up that before too long began to fight with one another.

Surely the priesthood would not have wished for their great knowledge to disappear forever. It is almost certain that they would have joined in the migrations, southwards towards warmer areas, that archaeology has shown took place around 1400 B.C.

Whatever knowledge they possessed it is doubtful if it had a place in a warmongering society. It is reasonable to assume that they would have travelled far and wide looking for a land in which to settle, whose inhabitants would accept and not abuse what they had to offer. Europe had become an unsettled place, although civilization remained around the Mediterranean. But of the lands in the Middle East, only in Akhenaten's Egypt would they have seen any sign of a peaceful, harmonious all-encompassing religion with which they would have had any empathy.

The most likely date for Akhenaten to have become pharoah is 1367 B.C. (7) His precise age on becoming king is not known, but he is thought to have been a young man. It was not long after he ascended to the throne that he announced a sweeping religious reform and replaced the supreme god Amon by the god Aten. This, however, was to cause far more upset than just annoying the priests of Amon. Amon had been simply one of the great many gods worshipped for various reasons throughout Egypt. As in later Classical Greece and Imperial Rome, there were many gods who had their individual jurisdictions over just about everything and anything we can imagine; besides which there were also many local gods worshipped in provincial areas. Amon was merely something like the father of the gods, as Jupiter would be to the Romans, or Zeus to the Greeks. We must not, therefore, assume there to have been a national Amon religion as such.

Aten was already a god in Egyptian religion, but Akhenaten did not simply proclaim him the supreme god, he proclaimed him the only god. Just prior to Akhenaten's time Aten was represented as a human being with a falcon's head, but after the first five years of his reign, Akhenaten replaced it with the Sun disc, its rays extending and ending in hands holding the Ankh (the symbol of life). No Egyptian god had ever been represented in so abstract a manner. Even the nature gods had been given a human body. Whether Akhenaten saw the sun as god in itself or as merely a visible symbol of god's all encompassing power is difficult to establish, but the abolition of Aten being represented in iconic form, and the idea of his omnipresence that we glean from Akhenaten's poems, has much in common with the later monotheistic religions of Judaism, Christianity and Islam. Whatever the true nature of Akhenaten's Atenism, it was a concept far in advance of its time — at least in the Mediterranean area — and would seem to have been the world's first recorded monotheistic religion.

What is certain about Akhenaten himself is that he had an unusually strong feeling for nature and all her creatures. He banned human sacrifices and even animals were no longer permitted to be hunted for pleasure. Other Pharoahs had always described them- selves as ferocious and vengeful, but Akhenaten broke from this tradition. Neither did he allow himself to be depicted in a military set- ting as did his predecessors and those who followed him on the throne of Egypt.

It is therefore not difficult for us to see why the Megalithic priesthood may have seen in Akhenaten the qualities they were looking for.

From the psychic messages we have received it is difficult to work out if Akhenaten's Atenism was the result of his being influenced by the Megalithic priests, or if they bequeathed him the knowledge once Atenism had been established.

Akhenaten built no stone circles, and it is impossible to say historically or archaeologically whether or not he had been influenced by the Megalithic peoples since we do not know what they believed. However, it must have been somewhat similar. The peace-loving ideals, harmony with nature, and exaltation of the sun, both have in common. The fact that Akhenaten never started a programme of stone-circle building is by no means indicative. If he had inherited the knowledge from the Megalithic priests, then it is logical to assume that the more advanced Egyptian technology would have made it unnecessary even had he incorporated their ideas.

The *malific force* (or intelligence) came into existence, so the psychic messages told us, with the last of the Megalithic peoples, and it appears that this above all other considerations was the reason why the Megalithic priesthood needed to pass on their knowledge. But what was this force, and how did it come to exist? Gaynor's automatic writings suggest that it was not a living intelligence — if *living* is the right word — as such, but more like a 'machine', similar to a computer mind. Exactly what this means we can only guess. However, we can perhaps make conjecture.

Imagine the Megalithic priesthood being called upon by the people of the British Isles to help them overcome their new hardships. Each individual tribe imploring their support, urging them to use what knowledge they may have possessed to protect them, to side with them and assail their enemies. Assume that their code forbade them to use their knowledge for military purposes, so the warriors took over where the priests had once resided. Perhaps some of the priesthood did attempt to use their power in this way. From Gaynor's writings we can deduce that this is what happened, and which created in some unimaginable way the *malific force* that was to remain. Somehow the priesthood prevented a repetition of the same thing. They sought a way of destroying this force and for this purpose eventually created the Stone.

As to where the Stone was fashioned, we have nothing tangible. We must suppose that the Megalithic people in the British Isles prior to 1500 B.C. were not responsible. The Green Stone is clearly not a natural formation. No such stone-cutting or working seems possible with what technology the Neolithic or Bronze Age people had, and no similar stones have been found here. On the other hand the Egyptians of this time had the means; in fact, many precious and semi-precious gems cut in similar fashion to the Meonia Stone originate from Ancient Egypt. (8) We can only surmise therefore that once the Megalithic priests arrived in Egypt they discovered that the advanced techniques used there enabled them to incorporate their knowledge in a more refined way.

As we have seen, some people suggest that the Megalithic stones held — and still do — strange powers that could be used for various purposes. Perhaps the priests were able to apply their knowledge and combine forces with the skill of the Egyptian jewellers. Perhaps they were delighted to find that they could utilize the properties of precious stones previously unknown to them. For it has long been believed that precious and semi-precious stones can hold magical power as talismans and amulets.

Returning once again to Akhenaten, why did he fail in establishing his new religion throughout Egypt? Instead of being exalted as a prophet, history laments Akhenaten as the heretic king.

There are a number of reasons why he failed. It was not only the bitter opposition of the priests of Amon that brought about his unpopularity. The whole Atenistic concept carried little weight with the mass of the Egyptian population fully content in their well-established traditions. To make things worse Akhenaten did nothing to increase his popularity by further isolating himself from his people. In the fifth year of his reign he moved his residence from the capital at Thebes to the new city he was building, Akhet-aten, meaning the place where Aten rises, and now called Tel-el-Amarna. Despite his ideals he considered himself as the only son of God, the chosen one for whom the entire world was created. The name he adopted, Akhenaten, means 'Incarnation of the Aten'.

But his chief failure was his neglect of the affairs of state. So much so did he ignore the events taking place in his country that he eventually made his son-in-law, Smenkhkare, co-ruler. As the years went by the empire that had been greater than ever before at the beginning of Akhenaten's reign began to crumble.

The priesthood, the noble families, but most importantly the army, finally refused to stand idly by and watch.

Eventually once the king had departed to his new city, the king's brother-in-law, Ay, probably the most powerful man in Thebes, decided to move against Akhenaten, and it was not long before he and his followers won Smenkhkare over to their side. There is much speculation about what actually happened next, because many of the inscriptions during Akhenaten's reign were later disfigured by the Amon priesthood. But it appears that Smenkhkare left Akhet-aten and went to Thebes where he was proclaimed sole king, and Akhenaten was deposed.

Akhenaten's fate is still something of a mystery. Some say he was poisoned, others that he went into exile, while there are those who believe that he was never, in fact, deposed.

Whatever the truth, it is certain that after reigning for seventeen years Akhenaten was no longer king. After his death or exile his religion was quickly abandoned by his followers, expecting reprisals, and the new city was left to crumble into dust.

It is at this point that we were told how a group of his followers, perhaps some of the original Megalithic priests, or their successors, returned to the British Isles where they founded a colony in what is now Central England.

Once again from a subsequent study of British pre-history, this decision to site their secret community in Central England appears feasible. If we look at a map of the British Isles showing the distribution of settlements and other 'ceremonial' sites during and just after the Megalithic period, we shall see that a large area in Central England was evidently unoccupied, mainly because at the time it was heavily forested. If they had to return to the British Isles what better place to suit their purpose, a central yet isolated position. Unfortunately, however, no Egyptian remains have yet been unearthed.

We next take up the history of this secret colony some centuries later, when we were told how some early Celtic migrants from Europe had joined them and thereby increased their numbers. We were informed that the colony had now been fortified and that a great warrior queen arose among them who built a powerful nation throughout Central England in order to safeguard their knowledge.

Once again the idea is possible. As we have already stated, the age of Berry Ring has not yet been established, but there are many such hill-forts throughout the country. Hill-top sites defended by banks and ditches that follow the contours of the hill are a classic feature of the Iron Age from 700 B.C. until the coming of the Romans in 55 B.C.

To find an approximate date for Gwevaraugh, assuming that she ever existed, it must have been some time after 700 B.C., since it was then that the Celts first arrived, although some authorities believe that earlier settlers had immigrated as early as 1300 B.C.

The original home of the Celts was what is now Bavaria, although there is also speculation that it could have been Hungary. From their home in Central Europe they spread westwards to the Atlantic coast and into Spain, then northwards into the British Isles. They came in small numbers until their major arrival sometime between 700 B.C. and 600 B.C., when they brought with them the Iron Age, and with it a more efficient means of waging large-scale tribal warfare. It would be reasonable to suppose that for Gwevaraugh to have been able to control such a large area she would have to have been aware of these new methods. If she existed, as we were told, then she would probably have established the powerful Cornovii tribe that had become well settled in the area by the time the Romans arrived. For these reasons a probable date for Gwevaraugh would be between 600—200 B.C.

Once again history can tell us nothing of Gwevaraugh or her feats. Prior to the arrival of the Romans there are no written accounts.

It is important now to examine the likelihood of a warrior queen leading a Celtic tribe. There have been renowned warrior women in history, Joan of Arc and the Saxon Queen Ethelfleda to name but two, but they are few and far between. One race in all history is unique in its tradition of women warrior leaders: the Celts.

The Roman writer Ammianus Marcellinus, in the 4th Century A.D. tells us that women took an active part in combat. Roman history recorded no male enemies in Celtic Britain to compare with the stature of Boudicca and Cartimandua.

Cartimandua ruled the Brigantes of the north, whereas Boudicca ruled the Iceni of Norfolk and East Anglia. And in Ireland too we have the legendary Queen Medb of Connacht.

Boudicca led a powerful rebellion in East Anglia in the 7th decade of the 1st century, and the Roman writer Dio Cassius gives us an impressive description of her.

She was huge of frame, terrifying of aspect, and with a harsh voice. A great mass of bright red hair fell to her knees, she wore a great twisted golden necklace, and a tunic of many colours, over which was a thick mantle fastened by a brooch.

History, tradition and legend alike echo the high prestige of women of Celtic mythology. There are the Celtic legendary Queens Scathach and Aife, as well as Gwenhwyfar.

In Irish and Welsh stories of Celtic Britain it was women who taught the great heroes both wisdom and the military arts.

Women also enjoyed an important place in religious life. Strabo, writing in 1st century B.C., reports that a community of holy women occupied an island off the mouth of the Loire from which men were excluded.

Not only women but the number *nine* figures strongly in Celtic religion. The idea of nine priestly women or maidens occupying secret places from where they hold on to an age-old mystical tradition is also reflected in classical writings. For example, the Roman geographer Ponponius Mela writing in the 1st century A.D., speaks of nine priestesses called the Gallizenae who possessed magical powers, and under a vow of perpetual virginity occupied an island at the western tip of Brittany.

So how far back did this unique tradition go? In the late 4th century B.C. the Greek writer Polybius says that the women accompanied their husbands into battle.

Some of the automatic writings of Gaynor indicated that this tradition of feminine equality in the Celtic realms came about *because* of Gwevaraugh.

We have already discussed the Knights Templar and the Gunpowder Plot. Beyond this further speculation is outside our briefing. Of the Order of Meonia which existed in the latter part of the last century we can make little comment. We were able to learn something of Mary Heath and Thomas Read, but more than this has not been possible.

Automatic writings have also referred to those who were involved but no further historical information has come to light. Nowhere have we found any records of the existence of this secret society. Neither have we found any direct connection between Thomas

Reade and Mary Heath. All we can say for certain is that they existed and were living at the same time, as was the gentleman connected with the Wolverhampton school. The people mentioned lived where we were told, and a mock Egyptian temple built in 1865 still stands in the grounds of Biddulph Grange. Unfortunately the temple does not constitute proof of the existence of a mystical order. Throughout the country there are many reproductions of ancient temples adorning the grounds of stately houses. Chinese, Classical, Gothic and other styles of architecture were a popular theme in the ornamentation of landscape gardening in the 18th and 19th centuries.

Perhaps, in the future, more light will be thrown on this peculiar history, but for the time being we shall avoid further speculation.

Appendix Notes

1 *The Prehistory of Europe*, Patricia Phillips, Penguin Books. 1981.
2 *View Over Atlantis*, John Michell, Abacus, 1973.
3 Pages 80-83, *Rings of Stone*, Aubrey Burl and Edward Piper, Frances Lincoln Pub. 1979.
4 *E.S.P. Beyond Time and Distance*, T.C. Lethbridge, Routledge and Kegan Paul, 1965.
   See also: *The Essential T.C. Lethbridge*, Tom Graves and Janet Hoult, Routledge and Kegan Paul. 1980.
5 *Needles of Stone*, Tom Graves, Granada. 1980
6 *The Flying Saucer Vision*, John Michell, Abacus, 1974.
7 *Chronology of World History*, G.S.P. Freeman Greville, Rex Collings. 1974.
8 See: *Jewels of the Pharoahs*, Cyril Aldred, Thames and Hudson. 1971.
   Egyptian Jewellery, Hamlyn. 1969.

Megalithic Period, Suggested Reading:
Megaliths and their Mysteries, Alastair Service and Jean Bradberry, Weidenfeld and Nicolson, 1979.
The Stone Circles of the British Isles, Aubrey Burl, Yale University Press, 1976.
A Guide to the Prehistoric Remains in Britain, Richard Wainwright, Constable, 1978.
Circles and Standing Stones, Evan Hadingham, Heinemann, 1975.
The Avebury Cycle, Michael Davis, Thames and Hudson. 1977.

Akhenaten, Suggested Reading:
Oedipus and Akhenaton, Immanuel Velikovsky, Sidgwick and Jackson, 1960.
Amarna, City of Akhenaten and Nefertiti, Julia Samson, Avis and Phillips, 1972.
Akhenaten and Nefertiti, Cyril Aldred, Viking Press, 1973.
Ikhnaton: Legend and History, Frederick John Giles, Hutchinson, 1972.
The Age of Akhenaten, Eleanore Bille-de-Mot, A. and M. Evelyn, 1968.

The Celts: Suggested Reading
The Celtic Realms, Myles Dillon and Nora Chadwick, Sphere, 1973.
Celtic Britain, Lloyd Laing, Granada, 1981.
The Celts, Nora Chadwick, Penguin, 1970.
Iron Age Communities in Britain, Barry Cunliffe, Routledge and Kegan Paul, 1974.
The Celtic World, Barry Cunliffe, The Bodley Head, 1979.

Index

Shotton, Pat, 76, 123, 128, 130, 137, 170, 171, 173, 175-6, 178, 179, 181, 188
Shotton, Terry (Biog), 10
Silbury Hill, 200, 201
Smenkhkare, 207-8
Smoke, strange appearances of, 116, 118, 119-20, 121, 170
Spirit Guardians of the Lights, *see under names of:*
    explanation of, 145
Spirit Guide to the Lights, explanation of, 145
Stafford Castle, 25
Standing stones, 110, 200
    see also Menhirs
Stone circles, 110, 152, 154, 200-1, 203, 204, 206
    see also under names of
Stone rows, 200
Stonehenge, 22, 197, 198, 200, 202
Strabo, 210
Studion, Simon, 193
Stukeley, William, 152, 201
Sub-Atlantic period, 203
Sub-Boreal period, 203
Sun Disc, Egyptian, 129, 131, 195, 205
Sunderland:
    Barry, 146
    Darren, 14
    Fred, 13, 15, 81, 112, 141, 172, 180
    Gaynor, UFO encounter, 7-8, 14
    Marion (Biog), 7

Swan, symbolic meaning of, 95-6
Swan's Neck, 95, 96, 97-104
Sword, The:
    age of, 126
    description of, 70-1, 74
    finding of, 66-71
    hiding of, 132
    message on, *see Meonia fore Marye*
use of, 91-2, 184, 187-8

Talismans, 207
Tape recording, unexplained, 19
Taylor, Carol, 157-8, 159, 160, 161
Tel-el-Amarna, 207
    see also Akhet-aten
Telepathy, 8, 190
Telephone, unexplained problems with, 173
Templars, *see* Knights Templar
Tennyson, 194
Thames, River, 147
Thebes, 207, 208
Thoth, 195
    see also Ape of Thoth
Tower of London, 36, 50
Trance, states of, 19, 21-5, 30-2, 77-8, 111-12, 113-14, 129, 167, 168, 171-2, 183-4
Tree of Life, 146

UFOs:
    encounters with occupants of, 6, 7, 14, 15, 110
    sightings of, 5, 7, 15, 109, 110

223